Whittington Castle: Outer gatehouse

THE CASTLES AND
MOATED MANSIONS
OF SHROPSHIRE

Mike Salter

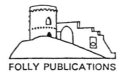

FOLLY PUBLICATIONS

ACKNOWLEDGEMENTS

The photographs in this book were taken by the author between 1969 and 2000. He also prepared the map and the plans, which are based on his own field surveys. Old postcards are reproduced from originals in the author's collection. Many of the plans are on a common scale of 1:800, but gatehouses and keeps are shown at 1:400 and large buildings and earthworks are mostly at 1:2000. Thanks are due to Mary Doncaster for transport and accommodation during work on this new edition. The proofs were checked by the author's mother Marjorie. Her brother, the late Roy Guest, farmed at Nine Springs, Clee Hill during the 1950s, and then lived at Howle, near Newport. Funds for printing this new edition were available thanks to a generous bequest in the will of Pat Baily, a cousin of the author's father Dennis Salter.

AUTHOR'S NOTES

This series of books (see full list inside the back cover) are intended as portable field guides giving as much information and illustrative material as possible in volumes of modest size, weight and price. As a whole the series gives a lot of information on lesser known buildings. The aim in the castle books is to mention, where the information is known to the author, owners or custodians of buildings who erected or altered parts of them, and those who were the first or last of a line to hold an estate, office or title. Those in occupation at the time of dramatic events such as sieges are also usually named. Other owners and occupants whose lives had little effect on the condition of the buildings are generally not mentioned, nor are 19th and 20th century events or ghost stories, myths or legends.

The books are intended to be used in conjunction with the Ordnance Survey 1:50,000 scale maps. Grid references are given in the gazetteers together with a coding system indicating which buildings can be visited or easily seen by the public from adjacent public open spaces which is explained on page 17. Generally speaking, maps will be required to find most of the lesser known earthworks.

Each level of a building is called a storey in this book, the basement being the first storey with its floor near courtyard level unless specifically mentioned otherwise.

Measurements given in the text and scales on the plans are in metres, the unit used by the author for all measurements taken on site. Although the buildings were designed using feet the metric scales are much easier to use and are now standard amongst academics working on historic buildings. For those who feel a need to make a conversion 3m is almost 10 feet. Unless specifically mentioned as otherwise all dimensions are external at or near ground level, but above the plinth if there is one. On the plans the original work is shown black, post 1800 work is stippled and alterations and additions of intermediate periods are hatched.

ABOUT THE AUTHOR

Mike Salter is 47 and has been a professional writer and publisher since he went on the Government Enterprise Allowance Scheme for unemployed people in 1988. He is particularly interested in the planning and layout of medieval buildings and has a huge collection of plans of churches and castles he has measured during tours (mostly by bicycle and motorcycle) throughout all parts of the British Isles since 1968. Wolverhampton born and bred, Mike now lives in an old cottage beside the Malvern Hills. His other interests include walking, maps, railways, board games, morris dancing, playing percussion instruments and calling dances with a folk group.

Shrewsbury Castle

CONTENTS

Inside the front cover is a map of buildings described in this book.

INTRODUCTION

Defensible residences of the type known to the Normans as castles were introduced to Shropshire after the Norman invasion of 1066. To control the Saxon town at Shrewsbury King William I "The Conqueror" in 1067-9 built there a new type of stronghold which the Normans had evolved. This castle was not constructed of mortared stone, for which years of peace would have been needed, but of earth and wood, which were quicker and cheaper materials to work with. It had an earth mound or motte surmounted by a tower with a small palisaded court around it, and there was a base court or bailey surrounded by a rampart and palisade with a ditch in front and containing a hall, chapel, stables, granary, workshops, and other buildings, all of wood. The tower on the mound formed a private dwelling for the lord (in this case the king) and a final refuge should the weaker bailey defences succumb to an attack.

In 1074 William I gave Shrewsbury Castle to a trusted comrade, Roger de Montgomery, who was made Earl of Shrewsbury. He was given a unusually compact group of estates and had special powers to rule Shropshire as one of a series of semi-independent counties forming a buffer-zone between the newly conquered English and the as yet unconquered Welsh. Shropshire also had a sheriff called Warin, who was married to the earl's niece and held a compact group of manors around Oswestry, but, like the other barons holding estates in Shropshire, notably the Corbets, Mortimers, de Lacys and de Says, he was subservient to the earl. These barons held their lands from the king in return for specified periods of military service by themselves and a specified number of knights, who were given units of land called manors to support themselves, this system being known as feudalism.

The veneer of landowning, French-speaking Normans consolidated their hold over the Saxon populace by constructing numerous motte and bailey castles with the aid of slave labour. The basic design varied according to the terrain, the labour and time available, and the other resources of the builder. A small enclosure with high earth ramparts (now known as a ringwork) was sometimes provided instead of a motte, and baileys were omitted or duplicated and made whatever size local circumstances dictated. Natural landscape features were utilised whenever possible, some mottes being natural hillocks with their sides steepened and the excess material used to form a high and level round summit. The Welsh Border Counties contain the highest concentration of motte and bailey castles in Britain, and there are about 75 of them in Shropshire. Most probably date from c1075 to 1100, although only three within the present county boundaries, Shropshire, Oswestry, and Holdgate, are mentioned in the Domesday Book survey of lands and their holders which William I commissioned in 1086. Other fine examples in the county of motte and bailey castles are Brompton, Clun, Hodnet, Caus, and The Moat, near Beguildy.

The Moat, near Beguildy

Quatford Motte

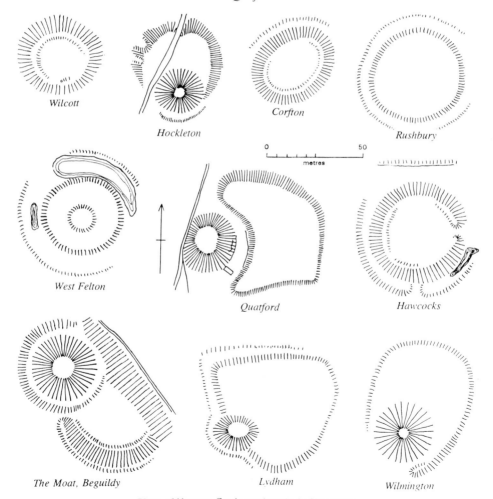

Wilcott

Hockleton

Corfton

Rushbury

West Felton

0   50
metres

Quatford

Hawcocks

The Moat, Beguildy

Lydham

Wilmington

Plans of Norman Castle earthworks in Shropshire

The Keep and Inner Ward at Ludlow

Roger de Montgomery added an outer bailey at Shrewsbury Castle and built new castles at Quatford, Ellesmere, Whittingdon and Hen Domen by Montgomery, the latter now being in Wales but included in Domesday Book as part of Shropshire. For in the 1070s Roger had ventured west over Offa's Dyke and the many modestly sized mottes around Chirbury and Worthen appear to be part of this campaign. Earl Roger probably gave land to trustworthy Normans on condition that they each built a fortified house on a motte of ordained size. The man-made layers have often now eroded and silted up the ditches so these mounds once looked more formidable than they do now. Most of them were abandoned as soon as stone castles and manor houses became fashionable but many of the Vale of Montgomery mottes still bore inhabited wooden houses in the 1220s when Henry III ordered them to be refortified whilst he was having a fine new stone castle constructed at Montgomery.

Timber is vulnerable to accidental or deliberate destruction by fire and soon rots away when in contact with damp soil. Gradually the most important earth and timber castles were rebuilt in stone. A few 11th century English castles were partly or wholly provided with stone defences from the beginning. One of the finest and best preserved of these is Roger de Lacy's castle of c1085-95 at Ludlow. It lies on a rocky site not so well suited for creating earthworks and has a bailey surrounded by a wall 2.4m thick and 8.0m high with an imposing gateway tower and four other square flanking towers, although, rather curiously, the side facing the approach has a blind spot left unflanked.

Roger de Montgomery died at Shrewsbury Abbey in 1094 and was succeeded in his English estates first by his younger son Hugh, killed fighting the Norsemen on Anglesey in 1098, and then by his elder son Robert de Bellesme. In 1101 Robert abandoned his father's castle at Quatford in favour of the larger and stronger site available nearby at Bridgnorth, where he may have closed off the tip of the promontory with a stone curtain wall. In the following year he sided with Duke Robert of Normany against the duke's younger brother King Henry I, who besieged and took the rebel earl's castles of Bridgnorth and Shrewsbury. These were subsequently maintained as royal strongholds.

Motte at Gwarthlow

Henry I appointed Richard de Belmeis, Bishop of London, as his justiciar and viceroy in Shropshire. He was invested with the authority of the former earl, but, being a celibate cleric, lacked dynastic ambition. Building in stone gradually became more usual in this period, although amongst Shropshire castles the only surviving masonry structure likely to be of Henry I's reign is the keep at Bridgnorth. In c1140 a very unusual round-naved chapel with an apsidal chancel was added at Ludlow. It is remarkable that such a fine structure was erected during the turmoil of the baronial revolts against King Stephen in support of Henry I's daughter Matilda. The castles of Shrewsbury, Ludlow, Ellesmere and Whittington were all held against Stephen when he marched through Shropshire in 1139. Shrewsbury Castle was stormed, but Ludlow was one of the strongest castles within Stephen's realm, and he failed to capture it. Although many earth and timber castles were built in England during Stephen's reign, Shropshire was already full of them, and only his supporter Hugh de Mortimer's castle at Cleobury is known to be a new creation of this period.

On his accession in 1154 Henry II sought to reduce the number of baronial castles, especially recently constructed strongholds in hostile hands. The rebel Hugh de Mortimer's castles of Cleobury and Bridgnorth were captured by the king in 1155. The latter was again retained as a royal stronghold but Cleobury was destroyed. The earthwork called Panpudding Hill lying opposite to Bridgnorth Castle across the Severn Valley Railway is probably a siegework constructed in that year, and Brockhurst Castle, which once had a stone curtain wall, is thought to have been built by Henry II during or immediately after this campaign.

Later in his reign Henry II had the hall and palisades of the inner and outer baileys at Shrewsbury rebuilt in stone, and he may also have erected a stone wall around the mound summit, thus creating what is now called a shell keep. Normally the central wooden tower would then be dismantled and replaced by lean-to wooden buildings set against the shell wall, but at Shrewsbury the tower apparently stood until c1270, when it and part of the shell wall and mound summit collapsed into the River Severn. Shell keeps were common in England and it is remarkable that although Shropshire has numerous mottes only that at Shrewsbury is known for certain to have had such a keep. The buildings upon the mound summits at Oswestry and Holdgate seem to have been rectangular rather than circular and probably totally roofed over, whilst walled courts on the large mounds at Clun, Bishop's Castle and possibly also Ellesmere were large enough to form inner baileys housing most of the principal buildings rather than just citadels or dwellings solely for their lords. This was also true of the shell walls erected on the ringworks at Corfham, Shrawardine and Tong.

The strong but comparatively small three storey tower keep at Bridgnorth, the earliest of several in Shropshire, is now thought to date from the 1120s. The middle storey contained the hall or main living room, at which level was the entrance, reached by an external stair. A spiral stair in one corner then led down to a dark storage basement and up to a private room and the battlements. It was probably towards the end of the 12th century that the Corbets built a large square keep at Pontesbury and a smaller one at Wattlesborough, the Le Stranges built a keep at Ruyton, and the de Lacys converted the gatehouse at Ludlow into a tower keep by blocking up the entrance passage and adding bed-chambers on one side.

Other tower keeps in Shropshire were probably built during the reign of King John (1199-1216). There was considerable opposition to the king from local barons and trouble with the Welsh in spite of John's illegitimate daughter Joan being married to Prince Llywelyn. The latter captured Shrewsbury in 1215, whilst King John swept through Shropshire in 1216, besieging the Fitz-Alan castles of Clun and Oswestry. The keeps at Alberbury and Whittington which lack the corner pilaster buttresses normally a feature of Norman keeps were probably built both by Fulke Fitz Warine during the period 1204-15 when he was at peace with King John. There are corner pilasters on the keep built by the Toret family at Morton, later held by the Corbets, who possibly had a fourth keep at Rowton. A square tower keep once stood in the inner ward of Bishop's Castle, whilst the remotely sited Fitz-Alan garrison post of Bryn Amlwg has footings of a circular tower keep probably the c1220s, and it is likely that another one stood on the mound at the principal Corbet seat at Caus.

The Fitz-Alan lords of Clun and Oswestry were descended from Alan, son of Flaad, a Breton given what had once been Sheriff Warin's estates by Henry I. This family indeed held the sheriff's office from 1155 until 1201, when they fell out with King John. Along with other Welsh Marcher barons they subsequently claimed that their lordships had been withdrawn from the ordinary county judicial system with the special status of "liberties" having their own military and judicial systems, a result of the need in these districts to concentrate military strength against the Welsh. This arrangement was only terminated when Henry VIII had the borders of England and Wales redrawn in 1536. Oswestry, Whittington and Clun then officially rejoined Shropshire whilst the lordships of Montgomery and Wigmore, once part of Shropshire, were given to Montgomeryshire and Herefordshire respectively.

Hall block at Stokesay

Wall-tower at Ludlow   *Shell keep footings, Shrewsbury*

Early in Henry III's reign further fortification against the increasingly united and belligerent Welsh became necessary. Walls serving also as barriers against vagrants wild animals and disease, and allowing the collection of tariffs on goods, were begun around the towns of Bridgnorth, Ludlow, and Shrewsbury. Licences were issued for the construction or remodelling of many castles. Since the anarchy of King Stephen's reign the crown had held a careful check on the building of private castles. All new work on fortifications was supposed to be authorised by a royal licence to provide crenellations (battlements). Receiving such a licence was a privilege and an honour. Crenellation thus became a status symbol and many of the later licensed buildings were show houses indefensible against a properly organised assault. However, the Shropshire castles built in the 1220s were very military in purpose and aspect. Fulke Fitz Warine added courtyards to his two new keeps at Whittington and Alberbury, the former having boldly projecting round corner towers and a wide water-filled moat. Round towers are characteristic of this period, as are entrances set between pairs of D-shaped towers. There are two such gateways at Whittington, although the much less substantially built outer gateway is probably of rather later in Henry III's reign. Footings remain of other gateways of this type at Bryn Amlwg and Shrawardine. Other works of this period were the outer bailey with round towers and a square gatehouse at Tong and the walls at Knockin and Corfham, all now vanished, the modest bailey wall at Moreton Corbet, the two round turrets at Clun, plus Red Castle, an unusual, enigmatic fortress sprawled across two sandstone ridges, on one of which was a small citadel with a well tower built up against the side of the cliff-face.

Inside the hall at Stokesay

The Fitz-Alan lords of Clun and Oswestry inherited Arundel Castle in Sussex in 1243 and were created Earls of Arundel in 1289, after which their influence in Shropshire declined. Around that time they built a lofty new solar block on the slope of the mound at Clun. The various administrative offices were held alternately by members of other baronial families like the Le Stranges, Corbets, de Audleys, de Somerys and Charltons. Changes were frequent, especially during periods of unrest like Henry III's power struggle with his barons in the 1250s and 60s, during which rebel barons captured Ellesmere and Bishop's Castle.

The town of Oswestry was walled in stone in 1277 on the orders of Edward I as part of his campaign against Llywelyn ap Gryffudd. With the prince's defeat and death in a skirmish near Builth in 1282, and the subsequent English occupation of North Wales, Welsh raids upon England came to a halt for a over century. The Welsh Marcher castles thus lost much of their purpose and their defences were allowed to decay. New castles built in Shropshire late in the 13th century and throughout the 14th century take the form of moated houses with comparatively thin walls and little or no provision for flanking fire, making them of minimal military value, although able to resist raids or burglary. New work at older castles in Shropshire during the reigns of the first three Edwards is mostly confined to domestic ranges and towers at Shrewsbury, Ludlow and Holdgate. Edward I built a new hall at Shrewsbury. Adjoining it are two round towers flanking the outer wall. In the early 14th century the Mortimers built a new hall and two fine suites of private chambers at Ludlow. These two projects are now almost all that are left of the domestic buildings of the 12th and 13th century castles in Shropshire. All the castles originally had numerous scattered buildings, chapels, kitchens, stables, etc, now only remaining at Ludlow.

The most famous, best preserved, and one of the earliest of the fortified manor houses of Shropshire is Stokesay. The hall and solar date from immediately after 1281, when the manor house was purchased by the rich clothier Laurence de Ludlow. This is a classic example of a prosperous tradesman seeking to join the ranks of the upper class by acquiring a symbol of lordly rank in the form of an embattled residence. For in 1291 Laurence was licensed to crenellate the house and he then enclosed the courtyard with a wet moat and an embattled curtain wall and built an impressive polygonal tower at one end. The crenellations on Robert Burnell's house at Acton Burnell, licensed in 1284, were just for show since the thinly-walled building had large windows at ground level and lacked the protection of an outer wall or moat. It is a hall-house with a hall and private chamber set end to end over basement rooms probably used as offices. The smaller hall-house of c1280 at Upper Millichope has thicker walls but has lost the battlements it is assumed to have once had. It housed an unpopular forest official in need of a stronghouse to live in. It contained a single living room set over a dark storage basement and is comparable with mostly slightly larger defensible hall-houses of South Wales, Northumberland, Scotland and Ireland. The rather more tower-like structures of the early 14th century at Lea and Hopton had similar arrangements, with probably only two storeys and perhaps an attic within the parapet. These follow the model of earlier keeps such at Moreton Corbet and Wattlesborough which originally only had two storeys. A further tower probably of this type, now vanished, is mentioned in 1283 at Meole Brace, south of Shrewsbury.

The NE part of Shropshire has fewer older castles but makes up for this with a series of 14th century moated houses. Myddle was licensed for crenellation in 1307, Dawley in 1316, Charlton in 1317, Apley in 1327 and the vanished mansions of Whitchurch, Withyford, Warrenshall, Sheriff Hales and the Charltons' town house in Shrewsbury were all given crenellation licences during the same period. Other moated houses at Stoke-upon-Tern, Leigh, Albright Hussey, and Stapleton are of late 13th or 14th century origin, and Cheswardine castle existed before 1330. Remains of these are minimal, comprising only the moats (drained in some cases), small standing fragments sometimes half buried in vegetation, and foundations. Enough remains to suggest that they were all rectangular with wide wet moats and plain, thin curtain walls surrounding modestly sized courtyards. None of them had a gatehouse of any consequence or any flanking towers, and in some cases the outer walls were not thick enough to support a wall-walk. The hall usually lay on the opposite side of the courtyard from the gateway and had service rooms on one side and apartments on the other. Cheney Longville, the best preserved house of this type, although the main hall is destroyed and the moat has been drained, was licensed as late as 1395. Sir Simon Burley's house of the 1380s at Broncroft seems to have been similar in layout to Acton Burnell, with towers set at the corners of a hall-block. As far as is known there was no outer wall, but it is likely there was a moat.

Lower Grounds moated site

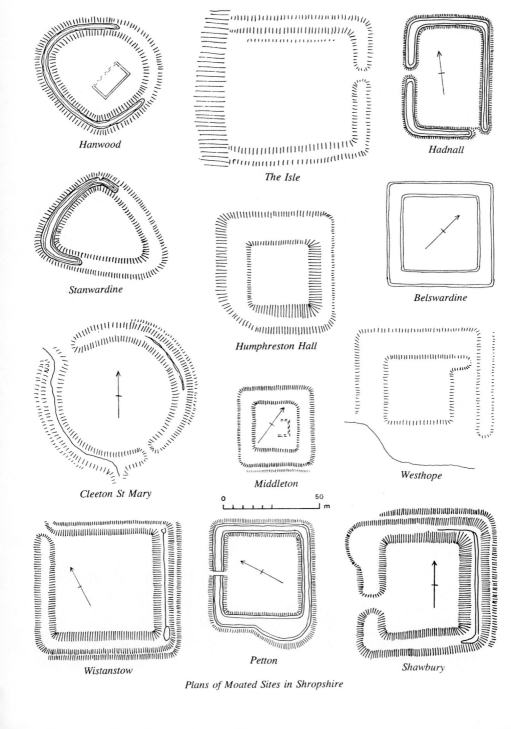

Hanwood

The Isle

Hadnall

Stanwardine

Humphreston Hall

Belswardine

Cleeton St Mary

Middleton

Westhope

Wistanstow

Petton

Shawbury

Plans of Moated Sites in Shropshire

Acton Burnell Castle from the churchyard.

Scattered across the county, but especially numerous in the flat NE quarter of Shropshire, are moated enclosures marking the sites of former manor houses. In most cases the buildings which stood inside these moats were purely domestic structures of wood, although a few have been superseded by farms of brick or stone in the 16th and later centuries. Most of the moats date from the 13th and 14th centuries, the most common form being a simple rectangular enclosure with a surrounding moat about 10m wide. The round enclosures near Great Hanwood and Soudley could be a slightly earlier type perhaps transitional from Norman ringworks. Only those moats threatened with destruction in recent years have been excavated, namely Shifnal, Watling Street Grange, Acton Burnell and Shackerley, remains of timber bridges being found at the last two. A moat was a permanent and efficient boundary for keeping vagrants, wild animals and malefactors out of manorial enclosures and would have been equally useful for controlling the comings and goings of domestic animals, servants and members of the family. At all times moats have been appreciated as scenic features and they served as a habitat for fish, eels, and water fowl which together formed a substantial part of the diet of the landed classes. A wet moat could also help to drain land otherwise unsuitable for agriculture or inhabitation. Moats were also sometimes used to flush away sewage, in which case a house built within one would require a separate source of water for cooking, brewing and washing, and also separate fish ponds. Because of the many uses to which they could be put, moats were not regarded as fortifications unless the area within contained a tower, curtain wall, earth rampart or a high palisade. Thus moats did not require royal consent of the kind required for the erection of embattled stone walls and towers. However moats still had a function as status symbols since only those who held manors or a considerable share of one had the resources to create them.

The words motte and moat clearly have a common origin. Modern historians understand them to mean quite different types of earthwork, a motte or ditched mound being a fortress but a moated site just an unfortified dwelling, but the distinction between the two is less clear in some old records. A dwelling of a person of middle rank stated to be on or in a "mote" in a 13th or 14th century document could refer to either type of earthwork. Also sites could change in status over the generations, a motte and bailey site later being downgraded to just a farm, or a moated site upgraded by the addition of a stone tower or a curtain wall.

In 1326 Edward II sought refuge from his enemies led by Queen Isabella and her lover Roger Mortimer, lord of Wigmore and Ludlow. The king was murdered at Berkeley in Gloucestershire in 1327 and his supporter Edmund Fitz-Alan, Earl of Arundel was taken prisoner by his own burgesses at Oswestry and executed at Hereford. In the early 1400s Owain Glyndwr led the Welsh in revolt against Henry IV and attacked Clun, Oswestry and Whittington. He failed to meet up with Hotspur Percy, heir of the Earl of Northumberland, at Shrewsbury in 1403, when the latter was defeated and killed by the royal army in a battle near of the town. Ludlow Castle passed from the Mortimers to the Dukes of York, whose influence in 15th century Shropshire was only rivalled by the Talbots, who succeeded to the extensive Le Strange estates in northern Shropshire in 1376 and, being staunch Lancastrians, were created Earls of Shrewsbury by Henry VI in 1446. When the royal army advanced to Ludlow in 1459 The Duke of York and his supporters fled, leaving the castle to be sacked. It became a royal castle when York's son Edward seized the throne in 1461. He had the keep remodelled and a new set of apartments built in the 1470s to accommodate his sons Edward and Richard, sent to Ludlow as figureheads for the newly created Council of the Welsh Marches. After their father died in 1483 the princes were sent by their uncle Richard III from Ludlow to the Tower of London and their mysterious deaths. Henry VII also sent his son Arthur with his new bride Catherine of Aragon to live at Ludlow. There the fifteen-year-old prince died in 1502.

In the medieval period castle walls of rubble were often limewashed outside, making them look very different from the way they do today. Walls built of limestone shale, a common building material in Shropshire, would tend to need an outer protective coat of rendering. Dressed stones around windows and doorways would usually be left uncovered. Domestic rooms would have whitewashed rooms decorated with murals of biblical, historical or heroic scenes mostly painted in red, yellow and black. Wall hangings decorated with the same themes or heraldry gradually became more common from the 14th century onwards. Although used in churches, glass was expensive and uncommon in secular buildings before the 15th century, so windows were originally closed with wooden shutters. These rarely survive, but original examples remain in the halls at Ludlow and Stokesay. As a result rooms were dark when the weather was too cold or wet for them to be opened for light and ventilation. Large openings in the outer walls sometimes had iron bars or projecting grilles even if high above ground level. Traces of these can be seen at Ludlow. Living rooms usually had fireplaces although some halls had central hearths with the smoke escaping through louvres in the roof. Latrines are common and indicate which rooms were intended for living or sleeping in rather than storage.

Furnishings were sparse up until the 15th century although the embrasures of upper storey windows sometimes have built-in stone seats, as in the halls at Ludlow and Shrewsbury and the living room of the stronghouse at Upper Millichope. Lords with several castles tended to circulate around them, administering their manorial courts and consuming agricultural produce on the spot. Seats belonging to great lords could be left almost empty when they were not in residence, unless a junior family member was installed with their own household. For much of their lives castles like Clun gradually crumbled away with only a skeleton staff to administer the estates. In times of crisis such as the Glyndwr revolt of the early 15th century the Crown sometimes had to order neglected castles to be repaired, provisioned and garrisoned. Servants travelled with lords and sometimes also portable furnishings such as rugs, wall hangings, cooking vessels and bedding, all kept in wooden chests. The lord and his immediate family plus honoured guests and senior household officials would enjoy a fair degree of privacy, having their own rooms. Servants and retainers enjoyed less comfort and privacy, sharing of beds and communal sleeping in the main hall and warm places of work like the kitchen and stables being common.

Wattlesborough Castle

The rebuilt gatehouse and a new domestic range at Moreton Corbet are the only noteworthy early 16th century works in any of the castles. Henry VIII's antiquary John Leland has left descriptions of many Shropshire castles which he visited during his travels in 1536-44. There are also a number of extant surveys from Queen Elizabeth I's reign. These are particularly useful for giving us an idea of what buildings once stood at Bishop's Castle and Bridgnorth, where little now remains of them. By Elizabeth's reign it was considered safe enough to pierce the thick walls of the inner bailey at Ludlow with large vulnerable mullion-and-transom windows serving the new ranges of offices and apartments built up against them. A fountain was provided in the middle of the bailey, whilst in the outer bailey were a tennis court, a new stable and porters' lodging, and a courthouse. Other works of this period on the castles were the building of a courthouse and new lodgings at Caus, repairs and additions at Bishop's Castle, repairs and a new upper storey to the hall at Shrewsbury, and the replacement of the medieval hall at Moreton Corbet by a stately new classical style mansion dated 1579.

Quite a number of places were garrisoned during the Civil War of the 1640s between King Charles and Parliament, despite the fact that by then many of the older castles were ruinous and the more recent fortified manor houses not strong enough to resist cannon of that period. The king visited Shrewsbury and Bridgnorth in 1642 soon after raising his standard at Nottingham. There were no great battles fought within the county, but the Royalists won skirmishes at Market Drayton and Lilleshall in 1644 and Knockin Heath and High Ercall in 1645, whilst the Parliamentarians were victorious at Montgomery, Norton and Whittington, and managed to capture Shrewsbury in a surprise night attack. A Parliamentarian news-sheet of 27th August 1645 lists Royalist garrisons at the castles of Bridgnorth, Broncroft, Caus, Dawley, Lee, Ludlow, Morton Corbet, Oswestry, Rowton, Shrawardine, Stokesay and Tong, plus the houses (most of them moated) of Albright Hussey, Atcham, Benthall, Buildwas, High Ercall, Lilleshall, Longnor, Madeley and Wroxeter. Of this period are the barbican and the postern tower at Shrewsbury Castle and the rough blocking up of various windows and doorways at Moreton Corbet. All these places were eventually captured although High Ercall held out until March 1646, Bridgnorth until April and Ludlow until the beginning of June. The castles at Ludlow and Shrewsbury were garrisoned throughout the Protectorate of the 1650s but later became ruinous. Other castles that were not already ruined before or during the fighting were slighted to prevent any future occupant of hostile Royalist garrisons.

In later years Stokesay, Cheney Longville and Upper Millichope became farmhouses, and the latter two still serve as such, whilst Stokesay is preserved as a monument in the custody of English Heritage, which also looks after the ruins of Acton Burnell, Clun and Moreton Corbet. New buildings incorporating some of the old parts were erected at Broncroft, Apley, and Tong, but of these only Broncroft still remains, and is now a private residence. The hall at Shrewsbury was patched up and inhabited in the late 18th century but was later purchased by the town and used for council meetings. The grounds of the inner baileys at Shrewsbury and Bridgnorth and the whole site at Whittington and the mound at Oswestry are gardens open to the public by their respective town councils. What little remains of the other castles and earthworks lie on private ground, although some can be seen from public places.

Town gateway at Bridgnorth

Window embrasure, Stokesay

GLOSSARY OF TERMS

APSE - Semi-circular or polygonal east end of a church containing an altar. ASHLAR - Masonry of blocks with even faces & square edges. BAILEY - defensible space enclosed by a wall or a palisade and ditch. BARBICAN - defensible court or porch in front of an entrance. CHEVRONS - A joined series of Vs forming a zig-zag. CORBEL -A projecting bracket supporting other stonework or timbers. CRENEL - A cit-away part of a parapet. CURTAIN WALL - A high enclosing stone wall around a bailey. EMBATTLED - provided with a parapet with indentations (crenellations). FOREBUILDING - A fortified porch defending the entrance of a keep. FOUR-CENTRED-ARCH - An arch drawn with four compass points, two on each side. GOTHICK - The imitation late medieval style of the 18th century. JAMB - A side of a doorway, window or opening. KEEP - A citadel or ultimate strongpoint. The term is not medieval and such buildings were then called donjons. LIGHT - A compartment of a window. LOOP - A small opening to admit light or for the discharge or missiles. MACHICOLATION - A slot for dropping or firing missiles at assailants. MERLONS - The upstanding portions of a parapet. MOAT - A defensive ditch, water filled or dry. MOTTE - A steep sided flat-topped mound, partly or wholly man-made. MULLION - A vertical member dividing the lights of a window. NAVE - The part of a church used by the congregation. PARAPET - A wall for protection at any sudden drop. PLINTH - The projecting base of a wall. It may be battered (sloped) or stepped. PORTCULLIS - A wooden gate made to rise and fall in vertical grooves. POSTERN - A back entrance or lesser gateway. QUOINS - Dressed stones at the corners of a building. RINGWORK - An embanked enclosure of more modest size than a bailey, generally bigger but less high than a motte summit. SHELL KEEP - A small stone walled court built upon a motte or ringwork. SOLAR - A private living room for the lord and his family. TOWER HOUSE - Self contained defensible house with the main rooms stacked vertically. WALL-WALK - A walkway on top of a wall, always protected by a parapet. WARD - A stone walled defensive enclosure.

PUBLIC ACCESS TO THE SITES   Codes used in the gazetteers.

E   Buildings in the care of English Heritage. Fee payable at some sites.
F   Buildings to which there is free access at any time.
H   Buildings currently used as hotels, restaurants, shops, etc.
O   Buildings opened to the public by private owners, local councils, trusts.
V   Buildings closely visible from public roads, paths, churchyards & open spaces.

FURTHER READING

The Castles and Old Mansions of Salop, Mrs F.S.Acton, 1858
Shropshire: Its early History and Antiquities, J.C.Anderson, 1864
The Country Seats of Shropshire, F.Leach, 1891
Antiquities of Shropshire, Rev Eyton, 1848.
Shropshire Houses Past and Present, S.Leighton, 1901
The Shropshire Landscape, Trevor Rowley, 1972.
Castles of Shropshire, Mike Jackson, 1988
Shropshire (Little Guides series) J.E.Auden, 1912
Shropshire (Buildings of England series) Nikolaus Pevsner, 1958
Transactions of the Salop Archeological Society.
Guide pamphlets are available for Acton Burnell, Ludlow, Shrewsbury and Stokesay.
For Ludlow Castle see also Archaeologia LXI, pp257-328.

GAZETTEER OF CASTLES IN SHROPSHIRE

ACTON BURNELL CASTLE   SJ 534019   F

Robert Burnell's hall-house at Acton Burnell is a castle in name only. It is crenellated (as licensed by Edward I in 1284) and has turrets but the walls are thin and have large windows close to the ground. There are no arrow-loops but there may have been outer defences since a stone gatehouse is mentioned in 1548. Burnell came from a minor family who were sub-tenants of the Corbets of Caus. He became a clerk serving Prince Edward, and was one of three proctors who looked after the prince's estates and interests whilst he was away on a crusade. Edward failed to get Burnell elected to the archbishopric of Canterbury, but he was made Chancellor in 1274 and in 1275 became Bishop of Bath and Wells. In the 1270s Robert Burnell rebuilt the church at Acton, his native village, and in 1283, perhaps before the hall-house was begun, he entertained the king and his court there. The parliament then held is said to have met in the great barn of which two gable ends remain standing near the 19th century hall. The great days of Acton Burnell ended in 1292 when Bishop Robert died. A lack of late medieval alterations suggests the building was little used after the last Lord Burnell died in 1420. The house passed to the Radcliffs and then to the Lovells by whom it may have been abandoned. They were forfeited in 1485 and Acton Burnell went to Jasper, Duke of Bedford, then in the 16th century to the Cromptons, whilst in the 17th century it was held in succession by the Hoptons, Haywards, Lees and Smyths. In 1660 the Smyths had ten hearths in their house here (a considerable establishment) but they seem to have abandoned it by 1672. The ruin was converted into a barn in the 18th century and two elliptical arches were inserted in the side walls to give access to the interior.

Acton Burnell Castle

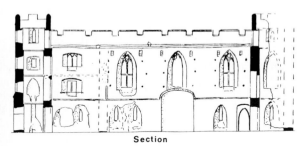

Section

CHAPEL

HALL

0   10

metres

STAIR

Plan and section of Acton Burnell Castle

Acton Burnell Castle

The ruined house resembles the hall of the walled and moated bishop's palace at Wells, also a ruin and the work of Robert Burnell. The house measures 23.1m by 16.4m over walls 1m thick. There are small square turrets at three corners, whilst the NE corner had a rectangular turret, now much ruined, containing a chapel on the second storey. Set between the western turrets is a rectangular latrine block, and between the eastern turrets was a service block containing a pantry, buttery and kitchen, all possibly timber-framed. On the SE turret are traces of the plaster which once covered the sandstone rubble walls both inside and out. Crosswalls divided the lowest storey into four rooms. The large SE room with two light windows, entered by a porch in the SE turret, was probably a hall for the bishop's household, with the smaller SW room a private chamber for his chief steward and having an octagonal vaulted strongroom opening off it within the SW turret. The NW room was probably a store and the NE room was a chamber or office, or perhaps a waiting room used by those requiring an audience with the bishop when he was in residence.

The eastern part of the upper storey formed an almost square state room or hall with lofty two-light windows with transoms and seats in the embrasures. In the east wall are two serving hatches flanking a doorway to the kitchen. One is now blocked by the reset piscina from the destroyed chancel of the chapel. The western part of the upper storey formed a suite of four chambers for the bishop, set in pairs on two low storeys together corresponding in height to that of the hall, connected by a spiral staircase in the SW turret, and provided with latrines in a block filling most of the west side. The lower northern room, opening off the hall, was the audience chamber. At the summit a narrow wall-walk with an embattled parapet led to the turret top rooms from a stair in the SE turret. In the 18th century a low-pitched roof was substituted for the original, which had two longitudinal ridges and a gully between. The battlements of the SW turret and west latrine block were then also replaced by pyramidal roofs which still remain.

Alberbury Castle

SECTION

STAIR

FIREPLACE

HALL

0   5
└─┴─┴─┴─┴─┘ m

DOORWAY

Plans of Alberbury Castle

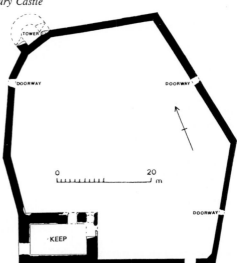

TOWER

DOORWAY   DOORWAY

0   20
└┴┴┴┴┴┴┴┴┴┴┘ m

DOORWAY

KEEP

ADDERLEY CASTLE   SJ 665404

A mound about 7m high is the sole relic of the castle of Nigel the Physician, who died in 1095. Adderley then went in turn to the sons of Roger de Montgomery, Hugh and Robert. After Robert's fall in 1102 Henry II granted Adderley to Alan de Dunstanville. The mound lies beside two ornamental lakes NE of the village and is known from excavation to have been occupied until the end of the 13th century. It has suffered from subsidence and now has an irregularly shaped summit 33m long, with an average width of about 17m. The house to the east may lie on the site of a bailey.

ALBERBURY CASTLE   SJ 357144   V

The rectangular keep here was built by Fulke Fitz Warine in the reign of King John as one of a number of strongholds protecting Shrewsbury from Welsh attacks. The bailey wall was added a few years after 1223, when the castle was captured and wrecked by Llywelyn Fawr, and has remains of one tower on the NW. The outer portion of the tower is destroyed but it was probably D-shaped like those at Fulke's other castle of Whittington. The castle lies so close to the parish church that there would not have been sufficient room for a NE tower to have existed. The saddle-back roofed church tower is built on the north side of the nave so as not to command the castle courtyard, but in any case it probably dates from the 1290s, by which time the castle was militarily redundant. The castle is thought to have been abandoned in the 14th century and was noted as a ruin by Leland, but there is evidence of the building having been renovated and occupied during the Civil War. The thin walling of the south and SE sides of the bailey seems to be of that period since the narrow SE doorway is dated 1646 on the inside tympanum. This doorway looks like re-used 12th century work and may have come from Shrawardine Church, which was dismantled in 1644.

The castle lies on almost flat ground lacking natural strength, and there are no signs of any ditches. The bailey wall is 1.6m thick above a battered base and still stands almost to the height of the wall-walk 4m above the courtyard. The NE and NW doorways look original, although much repaired, but the main gateway must have been in the south wall next to the keep, probably with an outer court beyond it. The very ruinous keep measures 16.9m by 11.3m over walls 2.5m thick above a chamfered plinth. It contained a storage basement at ground level, the north doorway of which may be original. The hall or living room above had its own entrance in the east wall and a fireplace in the middle of the north side. It does not appear there were any further rooms. The breach at the SW corner probably marks the position of latrines and there was a spiral staircase in the NE corner.

Alberbury Castle

ALBRIGHT HUSSEY   SJ 523176   V

This picturesque house, now a restaurant, consists of two parts leaning away from each other. The eastern half is a pretty timber-framed structure of two storeys dating from c1526 with probably later external decoration. The west part has two storeys of brick with an ashlar-faced third storey with mullion-and-transom windows. Inside it is a wainscoting panel inscribed "made by Edward Huse 1601". The southern approach to the house crosses by an old bridge the moat of an earlier mansion partly refilled with water to create a goldfish pond. The inner face about 1.2m high of the moat is faced with roughly shaped stone blocks. A depression marks the site of the moat on the north side. The last remains of a private manorial late-medieval chapel have now gone. In the early 17th century the house passed by marriage from the Husseys to the Corbets of Lee Hall and it was garrisoned by Sir Pelham Corbet for King Charles in the Civil War. Richard Gough in his "History of Myddle" records Sergeant Preece's defence of the house during a Sunday afternoon attack. The Corbets remained at Albright Hussey until they inherited the Sundorne estate in 1760.

APLEY CASTLE   SJ 656132   V

In the early 14th century the Charlton family was favoured by the Crown, Alan de Charlton being granted a licence by the young Edward III in 1327 to crenellate his mansions of Apley and Withyford. In the early 17th century a new three storey house with projecting wings was built for £6000 at Apley. An old sketch shows it enclosed a curtain wall (presumably older) with a rectangular gatehouse. This mansion still partly survives in a much altered state, having been adapted as a stable block of a new mansion, now demolished, built on the other side of the then one remaining arm of the moat in the 18th century. It is of grey ashlar with mullion-and-transom windows. It stands on medieval foundations and reset on the NW side is a medieval doorway. In 1643 Thomas Hanmer, who had recently married the widow of Francis Charlton, garrisoned the house for King Charles, but it was eventually captured, plundered of goods to the value of £1,500, and slighted by Parliamentary forces.

Albright Hussey

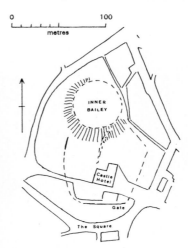

Plan of Bishop's Castle

BEGUILDY, THE MOAT   SO 188805

Lying just inside the Shropshire side of the border between England and Wales 1km NW of Beguildy is a well-preserved motte and bailey castle on a ridge rising 7m above a small stream which flows along the NE side and turns south to join the River Teme. The mound summit is 11m in diameter and rises 7m above the ditch. A D-shaped bailey extends 30m to the south and has on the SE and SW sides a rampart which is 1m high internally and 3m high externally.

BISHOP'S CASTLE   SO 393891   V

An early 12th century Bishop of Hereford built a castle in the NW corner of his large manor of Lydbury. There is a motte and bailey castle site called Bishop's Moat just inside Powys on a more commanding but also more exposed site 3km to the NW and the name Newcastle used in 1281 suggests a possibility that the early references are to a timber stronghold located there. The bishops seem to have later moved the seat of the estate further east, possibly in the 13th century, although the layout suggests a motte and bailey of 12th century type. When transferred by Bishop de Betun to the Mortimers in 1154 the main stronghold of this district was called Lydbury. The present site has been known as Bishop's Castle since 1285. After the defeat of Hugh de Mortimer in 1155 Bishop Foliot recovered his castle here and 20 marks were spent on fortifying it. It was in royal hands from 1208 to 1213. In April 1263 the Bishop was ordered to occupy the castle "for the better defence of the March in those parts. The castle armoury then contained 6 hauberks (protective tunics), 6 chapels de fir (iron helmets), and 6 balistae (crossbows). In July of that year the castle was stormed by John Fitz-Alan, Lord of Oswestry and Clun. The constable was killed and the town was occupied for 16 weeks, suffering much damage. Edward II forcibly occupied the castle unopposed in 1322 but later returned it to the bishop.

Bishop's Castle seems to have been kept in repair during the late medieval period since Leland described it c1540 as "well maintenid, and set on a strong rokke not very hi". An Elizabethan survey refers to 13 rooms covered with lead, 2 rooms covered with tiles, 2 more rooms in "le new building" situated on the outer wall between the gateway at "le prison tower", a tower on the outer wall containing a stable, and also a dovecote, garden, forest and park. In 1603 James I granted the castle to the Howards but they disposed of it in 1610, and in 1618 it was acquired by Henry, Earl of Arundel. By this time the building was probably ruinous and there is no record of it being occupied during the Civil Wars of the 1640s.

The castle site and remains are disappointingly unimpressive and difficult to distinguish from the gardens and back yards of the adjacent town buildings. The site commands an extensive view to the south and east but has no natural defences on the west and north, nor are any of the rock faces mentioned by Leland now visible. The Castle Hotel lies in the middle of the large outer bailey. Much of the southern wall survives hidden behind the shops on the north side of The Square. It acts as a retaining wall to a forecourt south of the hotel and seems to be about 4m thick, but is probably a stone faced earth rampart rather than solid masonry. In it, but difficult to see, is the bricked up outer gateway. On the west side near the mound it a small fragment of thin shale curtain walling 2.5m high above the present ground level to the wall-walk. Presumably there was once a deep ditch at a lower level outside it. A path from the back of the hotel leads up to the mound summit, now a bowling green about 50m across. It appears the mound has been lowered and levelled so the inner bailey lay at a higher level and was probably only about 35m across. The "prison tower" was probably the small rectangular tower keep which stood on the east side.

The leaning keep at Bridgnorth

The keep of Bridgnorth Castle

BRIDGNORTH CASTLE   SO 717927   F

In 1101 the noted military engineer Robert de Bellesme replaced his father's motte on a cramped site further down the River Severn by a new castle possibly of stone set on a sandstone promontory which may previously have been the site of a Saxon burgh or fortified town founded in 910 by Princess Ethelfleda. An old drawing shows the castle as having an ashlar-faced wall with a round arched gateway of three orders. In 1102 Henry I captured the castle from the rebellious de Bellesme and he later granted it to Hugh de Mortimer. On his accession in 1154 Henry asked Hugh to surrender his castles of Bridgnorth, Cleobury and Wigmore as a token of good behaviour, since de Mortimer had been a strong supporter of King Stephen. Hugh refused and fortified his castles against the king, who besieged and captured Bridgnorth in 1155. The royal Pipe Rolls record large sums spent on refortifying the castle in 1166-74, although there are no remains of this period since the keep is now thought to go back to the 1120s, despite similarities with Henry's keep at Peveril in Derbyshire. Henry II granted a charter to the town in 1157 and the High Street was laid out soon afterwards as a result of an outer bailey having been added to the castle on the site of the original trading centre of the town. In 1211-12 King John provided the outer bailey with a barbican and turning bridge. It stood near the Post Office, for the construction of which in 1901 a portion of the castle walling was destroyed.

Between 1216 and 1223 the town was surrounded by a ditch and turf rampart and after the rebellion of the 1260s the rampart was partly augmented by a stone wall. The castle was kept in repair until then but a report of 1281 lists many serious dilapidations. The main timbers of the floors of the keep had rotted because of the failure of the roof. The hall, chamber, kitchen and queen's chamber were all dilapidated, the stables had collapsed and the timber from them had been stolen, and it was unsafe to ride across the drawbridge on horseback. Repairs were probably carried out because Edward I was at Bridgnorth in 1294 and 1295. Edward II was here in 1321, recovering the castle from occupation by rebel barons, and again in 1326, whilst Henry IV paid two visits in the early 1400s.

In the 1540s Leland commented on the "2 or 3 strong wardes in the castle, that now goe totally to ruine". He says that the great gate on the north was blocked and replaced by an adjacent postern, and that the "castle ground, and especially the base court, hath now many dwelling houses of tymbre in it newly erected", proof that by then the town was encroaching upon the neglected fortress. The castle was still defensible, however, in 1642 when King Charles came to Bridgnorth at the start of the Civil War and admired the walks around the base of the walls with their fine views. He returned briefly in 1645. Parliamentary forces then blockaded the castle all through the subsequent winter and tunnelled under the walls, forcing Sir Robert Howard to surrender in April 1646. The castle was then dismantled.

All that remains of the castle is the keep, cracked and leaning dramatically as a result of being undermined and blown up in 1646. The southern half of the castle was divided by a north-south wall into an inner bailey on the east with the keep in its NW corner and a middle bailey to the west. An arch jamb with a portcullis groove adjoining the keep south wall was part of the gateway between these baileys. The keep measures 12.7m by 11.6m above a chamfered plinth from which rise corner pilaster buttresses. Most of the keep is faced with limestone but there are weathered sandstone blocks in the lower part of the north wall, which is 2.9m thick and without openings. The hall has a latrine in the NW corner and the west jamb of a fireplace in the south wall. It must have been entered by a doorway in the east wall, with a spiral stair rising up in SE corner, and probably also descending to the unlit basement. Above the hall was a low bedroom of which one jamb of a double-splayed west window survives. The roof sloped down from the east and west walls into a gutter drained presumably by an opening in the south wall. The battlements are destroyed.

The area of the inner and middle baileys now forms a public garden. The sheer cliffs on all sides except the north were more formidable before a road and various buildings were erected against them in the 19th century. The area of the outer bailey is now occupied by Georgian houses flanking East and West Castle Streets. The castle chapel of St Mary Magdalene was rebuilt as a parish church in 1792 to a design by Thomas Telford. Little remains of the town walls and of the five gates there now only survives the North Gate, most of which dates from a rebuilding of 1910. The Whitburn and Hungary gates were demolished in 1761 and 1821 respectively.

On the hillside SW of the castle at SO 715925 across the Severn Valley Railway station is Panpudding Hill. Similar to a number of siege castles built alongside major castles in the 12th century, it was almost certainly constructed by Henry II in 1155 to contain the movements of Hugh de Mortimer's garrison. It was used in 1645-6 as an emplacement for the besiegers' artillery. The earthworks comprise a ringwork 55m across with a rampart 3m high about the ground outside, plus a narrow bailey extending west for about 60m.

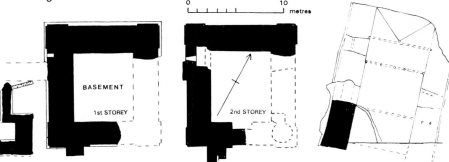

Bridgnorth: plans and section of keep

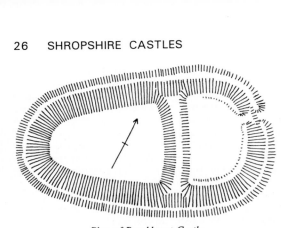

Plan of Brockhurst Castle

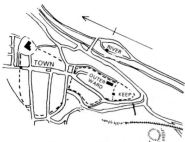

Bridgnorth: site plan

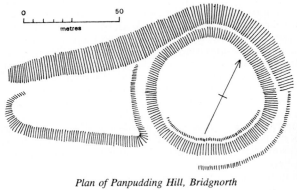

Plan of Panpudding Hill, Bridgnorth

The leaning keep at Bridgnorth

View across the Severn Valley Railway to Bridgnorth Castle

Brockhurst Castle

BROCKHURST CASTLE

This castle is thought to have been erected by Henry II in 1154-5 to help keep in check the rebellious Hugh de Mortimer. Custody of it was given to Engelhard de Pitchford, who assumed the name de Stretton and held it until the 1170s. Richard I had the castle repaired in 1194-5. The castle was repaired by Hugh de Neville, who was custodian from 1209 until he was forcibly ejected by John Fitz-Alan. Not until 1215 was he obliged to restore it to de Neville, who in turn was then ordered to hand it over to Hugh to Mortimer. In 1229 the castle was granted to Hubert de Burgh but it was forfeited on his fall in 1232 and then went to Henry de Hastings, who repaired it with timber from Womerton. The site seems to have been abandoned by 1255 when it was reported "there was no castle at Stretton". However "the ruins of an ancient castle called Brocard's Castle, were still remaining" as late as Camden's time, and an arch was still visible in the 19th century. There are still impressive earthworks of two baileys in line on a spur south of Church Stretton. The inner bailey at the SW end measures 60m by 40m and is known from excavations in 1959 to have had a curtain wall of local shale 1.8m thick from the start. It was partly buried in an earth bank and later completely robbed of its materials. A ditch 3m deep and 12m wide divides it from the D-shaped outer bailey 40m by 30m which has a rampart, and a deep ditch surrounds both baileys.

BROMFIELD MOAT   SO 479769

This moat may be the site of a castle of the Giffard family "by force razed" according to Leland, during whose time the farmhouse here belonged to the Earl of Oxford.

BROMPTON MOTTE   SO 545867   V

Behind a public house south of Brompton Hall, between the A489 and the River Caebitra, is a fine mound 8m high with a summit 9m in diameter. Part of the bailey platform to the SE was removed in the 19th century for the construction of a mill pool, now dry.

BRONCROFT CASTLE   SO 545867   V

The ruinous circular structure in front of this building may be a corner tower or a dovecote (the latter is more likely), belonging to the castle or house which Roger Tyrell is said to have had at Broncroft in the early 14th century. The Burley family obtained Broncroft c1361 and the oldest parts of the present house were begun in 1382 by Sir Simon Burley. One of the chief captains serving under Edward III's son Edward the Black Prince, Burley was to tutor to Prince Edward's son who suceeded his grandfather as Richard II in 1377. Unpopular because of his influence on the king (who was still a minor), Burley was disgraced and unjustly executed in 1386. His family retained possession of Broncroft until at least the 1450. The castle then passed first to the Chetwynds and secondly to the Littletons. Leland called Broncroft "a very goodly place like a castle" c1540 and by that time it was a possession of the Talbot Earl of Shrewsbury. By the end of Elizabeth I's reign Broncroft had passed to the Lutleys of Enville. The castle held a Royalist garrison in 1642 but but by 1645 was held for Parliament by Lord Calvin. In July of that year a troop of Royalist horse defeated the garrison outside the castle, many being killed and wounded and 50 taken prisoner. In July 1648 Parliament gave the order to "demolish Broncroft Castle and make it untenable", but the Lutleys later patched it up and continued to live there. They changed their name to Barneby in the 18th century and in 1807 sold Broncroft to the Boyds of Rochdale. The house was rebuilt in the 1820s after being purchased by George Johnstone. It passed to the Stutfields and was then sold in 1889 to James Whitaker, who erected much of the present building, including the entrance with false machicolations above it. During the 20th century the house was occupied by the Pembers and Brinton families.

Broncroft Castle

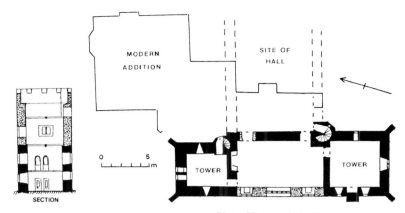

Plan of Broncroft Castle

Although little remains of it, the castle as rebuilt by Sir Simon Burley was an unusual building. The southern of the two surviving towers measures 7m square over walls 1m thick which are original only in the lowest storey, and even there provided with a 19th century plinth and windows. The room has no direct access to a stair in a turret in the NE corner. Just 9.2m to the north is a second tower measuring 6.5m by 5.7m externally. The two lowest storeys have pairs of narrow windows set oddly close together probably serving latrine closets. The third storey, the battlements, and most of the stair turret at the SE corner are 19th century. Between the two towers, and with a rebuilt west wall flush with their west walls, was a block containing the main private chamber on the second storey with a chamber or office for a household official below it. East of the original wall connecting the two tower staircases there extended a block which contained the main hall over offices or storerooms. From the hall direct access could have been possible via the staircase to a third storey bedroom of the SW tower. Probably there were two more square towers at the east end, making an H-shaped plan, recalling not only Acton Burnell not far away but the layout of the 14th century tower houses of Harewood and Langley in Northern England, and the keep at Stafford, where the corner towers are octagonal instead of square.

BURFORD CASTLE   SO 581679

The existing red-brick mansion built by William Bowles is dated 1728 on a drainpipe. During demolition of two later wings in the early 20th century remains were found under the west wing of what is thought to have been a moated manor house of the Cornwayle or Cornwall family, several of whom are commemorated by effigies dating from the 1370s to the 1580s in the parish church. The site lies by the River Teme.

CALLOW CASTLE   SJ 380049

An Iron Age hillfort 160m long by 120m wide upon Callow Hill seems to have been adapted in the early 13th century as a castle by the Corbets of Caus. The only mention of the castle is in a charter of the 1270s. It seems to have had stone defences, parts of which remained in Leland's time, but were said to have been removed in 1688 for making the foundations of the new church at Minsterley.

CASTELL BROGYNTYN   SJ 274314

On a spur above two ornamental lakes west of Oswestry is a ringwork about 45m across with a rampart 1.5m high above the interior and over 4m high above the surrounding ditch, which has an outer bank. The interior was used as a bowling green in the early 20th century but is now planted with trees, whilst the outer banks are very overgrown. The castle was probably built by Owain Brogyntyn, who died c1205, as a Welsh response to the fortifications at Oswestry.

CASTELL BRYN AMLWG   SO 167846

In a remote position in the western edge of Clun Forest is a knoll with steep slopes to the north and west and marshland on the other sides. The knoll has been scarped into a ringwork 47m long by 28m wide with a ditch and an outer bank. Nothing is known for certain about the history of this site but thanks to excavations in 1963 much can be conjectured. It must have been an outpost of Clun marking the otherwise uncertain border between Shropshire and the Welsh district of Maelienydd and is likely to have been created by Helias de Say c1142 after he slew two of the sons of Madog ap Idnerth of Maelienydd. At the south end are traces of the footings of a round tower keep, shown by excavation as being nearly 11m in diameter over walls 2.4m thick. The bailey wall built in long straight sections about 1.8m thick was contemporary as it had a latrine shute serving an upper storey of the keep. Both were probably built by John Fitz-Alan, Lord of Clun from 1215 to 1241. At the north end are traces of a gatehouse with a passage about 2m wide flanked by rectangular guard rooms with round fronts towards the field. This gatehouse and the small, perhaps solid, D-shaped towers added to the middle of the east and west sides of the bailey wall could have been built by Llywelyn ap Gruffudd in the 1260s or 70s but are more likely to have been added by the Fitz-Alans to strengthen the castle against this Welsh prince in the last few years before he was killed at Builth in 1282. With the Fitz-Alans transfer to Sussex shortly afterwards it is unlikely the castle saw any subsequent use. It does not appear to have had any accommodation other than the four or five rooms which would have been available in the upper parts of the gatehouse and keep. The NE corner of the enclosure has been damaged by quarrying for roadstone, the outer bank having been breached to give better access.

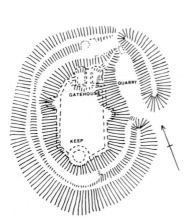

Plan of Bryn Amlwg Castle

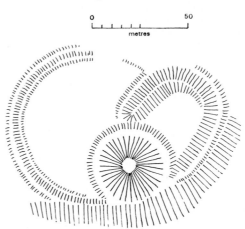

Plan of Castle Pulverbatch

Remains of the gatehouse at Bryn Amlwg Castle

CASTLE PULVERBATCH   SJ 423022   F

The castle is assumed to have been built by Roger Venator, who held the manor in 1086. It is first mentioned in the 1150s when it was held by Herbert de Castello, who had married the heiress Emma de Pulverbatch. It then passed to the Kilpeck family but William de Cantilupe had custody of it during the long minority of Hugh de Kilpeck for much of King John's reign. Hugh's heiress married Philip Marmion, and a "capital messuage" is mention in the inquisition after Philip's death in 1291, when Pulverbatch passed to his nephew Ralph Boteler. The site may have remained occupied throughout the 14th century, the castle chapel being mentioned in 1427.

There are no signs of any stone buildings despite long occupation of the site, but impressive earthworks lie on a hillside at about the 230m contour with a steep drop to a stream on the south. The motte rises 8m to an uneven summit 13m across and has to the NE a quadrangular bailey about 30m across with a rampart on the north side rising 1.5m above the interior and 3m above the ditch. Facing the higher ground to the west is a semi-circular outer bailey about 75m across with a rampart and ditch.

Castle Pulverbatch

CAUS CASTLE

The 37m diameter ringwork NE of Hawcocks Farm at SJ 349078 was probably erected by William Corbet in the 1070s, the name Caus deriving from his estate in Normany of Pays de Caux. It has a rampart over 5m high above a still partly water-filled ditch and 1.5m high above the interior. Roger Corbet was forfeited for his part in Robert de Bellesme's rebellion in 1102 but was restored to his estates c1115. It was probably he who transferred his seat from Hawcocks (which more directly commands access up the valley) to the stronger site on the hill above where there may have already been earthworks of an Iron Age fort. The castle was so important for the defence of the border that the Crown took an interest in its maintenance, Henry II having it garrisoned in 1165 during a Corbet minority, and Richard I contributing 10 marks in 1198 towards building work by Robert Corbet which may have included walling the bailey in stone. Henry III granted £20 in 1225 and 50 marks in 1263 towards further work on the defences by Thomas Corbet which are likely to have included D-shaped flanking towers. In the 1320s Caus passed by marriage to the de Leybournes and then in 1347 went to Ralph, Lord Stafford. The two town gateways are mentioned in 1371, and several towers are mentioned in connection with the expenditure of £22 on repairs c1399. Caus was garrisoned against the rebellions of Owain Glyndwr in the 1400s and Sir Gryffudd Vaughan in 1444 but the Staffords by then only used the castle as a prison and administrative centre. The castle was described as "in great ruin and decay" in a survey of the recently executed Duke of Buckingham's estates in 1521. Lord Henry Stafford built a new house in the bailey in the 1550s and a courthouse was built within the barbican. Lord Stafford sold Caus to Sir Rowland Hayward in 1573 but the Staffords appear to have remained in possession until Hayward's son-in-law John Thynne seized it by force in 1590. On his death in 1604 the castle seems to have been in reasonably good repair and in the 1630s the Thynnes spend over £800 on additions and repairs. In 1645 the castle surrendered to a Parliamentary force after a short siege and was then dismantled. Some fittings were transferred to Minsterley, where the Thynnes later lived. The ruins were used as a quarry for road stone during the 18th and early 19th centuries but much masonry still remained until the 1830s.

Just 1km SW of the castle is Lower Wallop Farm, where the Moat Field SW of the house may be the site of the "moated capital messuage with a dovecote" mentioned in 1381. The ditch of Wallop Castle is mentioned in 1350. This site was perhaps the home of an important estate official.

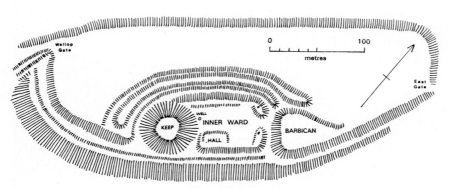

Plan of Caus Castle

West or Wallop gateway at Caus

Caus has one of the best defensive sites along the whole Welsh Border and by the end of the 13th century this was a very strong castle indeed. Steep slopes fall away from both sides of the ridge. The sole relic of the walls of the outer bailey which actually enclosed a small town is one side of base of the Wallop Gate at the SW corner. The inner bailey and motte are overgrown, covered with trees, and buried in the debris of their own walls. Considerable amounts of masonry lie buried and there are fragments still standing quite high up, but again half buried, of two D-shaped towers flanking a gateway at the NE end. A platform on the SE side is the site of a large hall, NW of which, at the foot of the mound, is a stone-lined well shaft. The NW side of the bailey has a formidable double ditch and rampart system. The motte rises steeply to a summit over 12m above the ditch to the SW. There are no certain remains of the shell keep described by other writers and the surviving fragment on the mound summit, although possibly not medieval in its present form, suggests a round tower keep about 11m in diameter. An old drawing of the castle shows a round tower keep on the mound summit and two baileys with round flanking towers.

CHARLTON CASTLE   SJ 597112

In 1317 Edward II licensed John de Charlton, Lord of Powys, to crenellate his house of Charlton. In the middle of the 16th century it passed to Jane Orwell. The remains comprise a platform 70m long by 50m wide rising about 2.5m above the bottom of a moat 17m wide which is still filled with water except on the NW side. The remaining fragment of sandstone walling 1.1m thick and 3m high was presumably part of the inner wall of the hall on the SE side. Only buried footings at the north and south corners, and fallen fragments near the east corner, remain of the curtain wall. The gateway would have been on the NW side. opposite the hall, where there is a causeway across the moat.

Cheney Longville Castle

CHENEY LONGVILLE CASTLE   SO 418849 & 417848

Longville was originally held by the Burnells but the Cheneys were in possession from the early 14th century. With the fork of roads at the top of the village is a worn-down oval ringwork with a rampart now 2.5m high measuring 56m by 32m across. In 1395 Richard II licensed Sir Hugh Cheney to crenellate the existing castle further south. It passed to the Plowdens in the 15th century and to the Beddoes family in the 18th century. The pair of cannon balls at the castle appear to be relics of a bombardment by Parliamentary forces during the Civil War. The north corner is now occupied by a farmhouse which appears to be a 19th century remodelling of a late 17th century or 18th century structure built up from the still surviving base of the medieval outer wall. The remainder of the castle serves as a farmyard with agricultural implements and livestock occupying the slowly decaying buildings.

The castle consists of four comparatively narrow two storey ranges set round a courtyard 32m long by 17.5m wide. Even with the moat drained and the upper parts of the walls rebuilt without their crenellations Cheney Longville is better preserved than the other 14th century stronghouses in Shropshire and gives some idea of what they looked like. With walls only 1m thick without any flanking towers the castle was never of any significant military strength. The three surviving original ranges contain several narrow windows and some old doorways but have been much altered. None of them seems wide enough to contain the main hall, which must have been in a range on thje NE side wider than the farmhouse now occupying the northern half of this side. The NW range contains the gateway, flanked by rooms for porters or guards without any defensive features to the flat-ceilinged passageway. The decayed rooms above are partly reached from within the farmhouse and partly by an external stair in the west corner. The only notable features are a doorway with a 14th century type shouldered lintel and the roof with trusses and queen-posts. Only the western two thirds of the SW range survive. The cross-walls are not old, except for one near the south end with two blocked original doorways. The thin inner wall of the SE range looks much rebuilt but contains original doorways. The centre part of this range projects slightly towards the moat and has two lancet windows at a level intermediate between the levels of the other windows of the two storeys. Further south in the outer wall is a blocked plain mullioned window, probably 17th century.

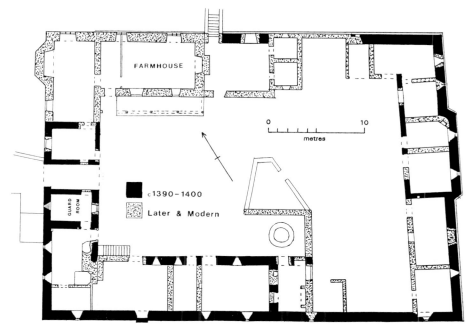

Plan of Cheney Longville Castle

Cheney Longville Castle

Cheney Longville Castle

Cheney Longville Castle

*Cheney Longville:
section of SE range*

CHESWARDINE CASTLE   SJ 719301

The manor of Cheswardine was held by the Le Strange family from 1160 until the death of John de Strange in 1330, when a survey of his estates noted that the castle was of little strength. It was probably built by John, who obtained a charter for a weekly market in the village in 1304. All that remains is a moat containing water about 8m wide enclosing a platform 47m by 44m. The moat has a wider section at the SW corner and is crossed by a low causeway on the south with traces of a second of the north. Nothing is known of presumed stone defensive walls or of the internal buildings, which were perhaps wooden framed.

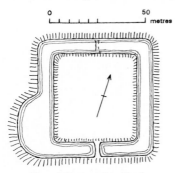

Plan of Cheswardine Castle

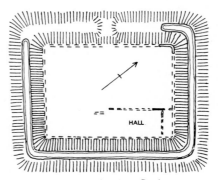

Plan of Charlton Castle

Moat of Cheswardine Castle

CLEOBURY MORTIMER   SO 683758 & 674757

A castle here is first mentioned in 1154 when Hugh de Mortimer fortified his strongholds against Henry II. The wording of Camden's description of what even in his day were meagre remains suggests the castle had been built by Hugh in the 1140s. It was soon captured and destroyed but is said to have been rebuilt in the late 1170s. There are two possible sites, one immediately north of the parish church, the other is a semi-circular ringwork 60m by 30m above the east bank of the River Lea, 1km east of village, with a rampart rising 3.5m above a ditch with an outer bank, and now containing a house of the 1950s. The reports of fragments of walls and foundations being visible in the late 18th century may have applied to either site.

Clun Castle mound

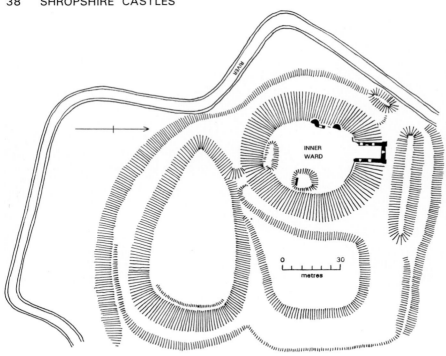

Plan of Clun Castle

CLUN CASTLE   SO 299809   F

Robert (better known as Picot) de Say, who died d1098, is credited as having built this castle. In the mid 12th century Clun passed by marriage to the Fitz-Alans, and they held it until the 1540s when the then ruinous castle passed to Thomas Howard, Duke of Norfolk. In 1195 the castle was stormed and burnt by the Welsh leader Prince Rhys prior to his victory at the battle of Radnor. Rebuilding in stone probably then followed. The castle is said to been besieged by King John in 1216 and in 1234 the Welsh burnt the town, although the castle held out. The feeble ringwork at SO 290785, 2.5km to the south of the castle may have been the site of a siege camp during one of these campaigns. An inquisition into the estates of John Fitz-Alan on his death in 1272 refers to Clun Castle as being small but well built, suggesting that only the motte ever bore a stone wall. There was an incomplete gatehouse and in the bailey were a grange, stable, and bakehouse, all in a "weak state". The impressive keep-like block built against the north slope of the motte may be of the period immediately after this survey and the tower then in need of a new lead roof could have been the structure of which a fragment remains on the east side of the mound summit, possibly a tower keep of c1200. The castle is said to have been attacked by Owain Glyndwr in the early 1400s but with the pacification of Wales, and the continued absence of the Fitz-Alans at their much grander and less remote seat of Arundel in Sussex, the castle at Clun was allowed to decay. The Howards later sold the site to the Earl of Northampton but in the 1890s repurchased it as a reminder of their past. The ruins have long been freely accessible to visitors and are now in the custody of English Heritage.

The earthworks comprise two baileys lying east of a large and high mound probably mostly natural. A ditch surrounds the whole and just beyond the shallow River Clun gave some extra protection on the west and south whilst on the north there is a high outer rampart and ditch with marshland beyond. The north bailey is now used as a bowling green. A causeway connects it with the south bailey, which has a rampart on the east and is itself connected to the mound by another causeway.

The mound summit bore a curtain wall enclosing a court about 51m long by 36m wide. The only remaining fragment lies on the west side. It contains one embrasure and connects two solid semi-circular turrets. On the east side is a low fragment and the buried base of what appears to have been a tower about 10m square, possibly a keep like that at Wattlesborough. The principal remaining structure on the mound is a block built against it so that the two lowest of its four storeys were below the mound summit. Although usually described as a 12th century tower keep until fairly recently, this building is now thought to be of the 1260s or 70s. It measures 11.8m over side walls 3m thick and was over 21m long, but the south wall towards the motte summit is now entirely destroyed. It must have contained a lobby connecting the entrance with passages and stairs to the three upper levels. The north end wall has a battered plinth and rises up from the motte ditch in a most impressive manner. Square turrets clasp the corners and contain small rooms higher up. The lowest level was a dark storeroom with a straight mural stair rising up from one side of a postern in the west wall. The second and third storeys were public rooms with fireplaces in the west wall and pairs of windows on each side with seats in the embrasures. The ruinous topmost storey was the lord's private room and has a fireplace in the east wall. This building makes an interesting comparison with the two storey hall block perched on one side of the motte summit at Grosmont in Gwent and with some of the two storey mid 13th century hall keeps in Ireland like Clonmacnoise and Greencastle which also have square turrets clasping their corners.

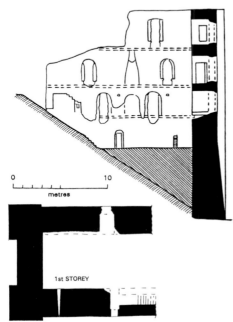

0   10
metres

1st STOREY

Solar block at Clun; plan and section

The solar block at Clun

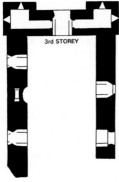

Clun: Interior of solar block

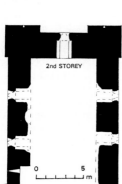

*Plans of the
solar block at Clun*

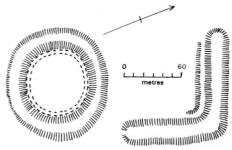

Plan of Corfham Castle

CORFHAM CASTLE   SO 525850

Corfham was granted by Henry II to Walter de Clifford, father of his favourite mistress the celebrated Rosamund. The castle is first mentioned in 1233 when it was confiscated by Henry III after the third Walter de Clifford rebelled against him. In 1271 Corfham passed by marriage to John Giffard of Brimpsfield in Gloucestershire. On his death in 1299 the castle was said to be so ruined as to be of no value. However it seems to have been repaired after it passed by marriage to Fulk Le Strange. The castle chapel and its chaplain are mentioned in a document of 1384. A 16th century account says that "Corfham hath been a manor of great fame, and hath in it a castle compassed about with a mott (moat) and a strong court wall, strong towers, whereof one doth remain called Rosamund's tower but can't stand for long for it is uncovered and the lead taken away". The foresaid court was also compassed about able to withstand any suddain invasion, but now all decayed, ruinated and destroyed. Lying on level ground is an oval ringwork with a bailey to the north. The ringwork bank covers the footings of a curtain wall around a court 30m across. The wall and its reported towers were probably built in the 1220s, the likely date of Walter de Clifford's other castle of Clifford, east of Hay-on-Wye.

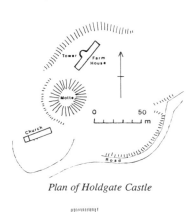

Plan of Holdgate Castle

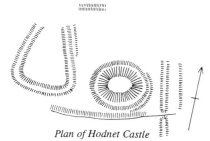

Plan of Hodnet Castle

Holdgate Castle

HOLDGATE CASTLE   SO 562897

Holdgate or Stanton Holdgate is named after Helgot, who was given the estate by William I. His motte and bailey castle here is one of the few in Shropshire mentioned in the Domesday Book survey of 1086. His son Herbert Fitz Helgot succeeded in 1087 and entertained Henry I here in 1109. During King John's reign Holdgate passed to the Mauduits. It was confiscated in 1216 but restored to them by Henry III in 1217. The castle was transferred to the king's brother Richard, Earl of Cornwall, in the 1250s. The castle is said to have been ruinous when purchased in 1284 by Robert Burnell, Bishop of Bath and Wells. He is said to have built the D-shaped tower which projects from the NW side of the present farmhouse, yet on his death in 1292 the "old castle" is said to have been "of no value". Holdgate passed to the Radcliffs in the 1420s and then went to the Lovells until they were forfeited in 1495. It was granted by Henry VIII to the Duke of Norfolk, exchanged in 1543 with Sir John Dudley, and then passed to the Cressets. A brick tower is mentioned in 1644 when the castle was besieged by the Royalists.

The castle stands high on a hill above Corve Dale and has an overgrown motte rising 7.5m to a summit 18m across on which are footings of a building, supposedly rectangular, although clearance would be required to prove this, and probably a keep built by the Mauduits. The mound lies within the western side of a large bailey platform about 100m across. It is possible that only the northern half of this, in which lie the farmhouse and tower, was walled. The tower is about 8m in diameter and has two storeys, rising 10m to the eaves of the present semi-conical roof. There are slits with top and bottom roundels suggesting a 13th century date, but the building seems to have been refaced some time during the 19th century.

HOPTON CASTLE   SO 367779   V

Hopton originally belonged to the de Says as part of the lordship of Clun but by the mid 12th century had passed to Osbert de Hopton. The last de Hopton, Sir Walter, d1305, was a man of some consequence and the towers whose buried footings survive at the SE, NE, and SW corners of a roughly rectangular bailey may be of his period, unless they go back to the period around 1231 when Henry III may have briefly stayed here. The site recalls the layout at Skenfrith, Gwent, built around that time. In 1267 a complaint was made that in November 1264 Walter de Hopton had seized £20 worth of cattle and taken them to his castles at Hopton. This suggests that the present site had been fortified by then and that perhaps the small ringwork at Warfield Bank (SO 371774, 37m in diameter with a rampart up to 2.5m high) was also then in occupation. The keep seems to be a 14th century addition and has earth piled against its base so that it appears to stand on a small motte. The castle passed by marriage to the Corbets in the mid 15th century and was sold during Henry VIII's reign to the Wallops. In 1643 Henry Wallop installed a Parliamentary garrison of 31 men under Samuel More. Early in 1644 Sir Michael Woodhouse brought up a Royalist force which breached the bailey wall and burnt the porch of the keep. The garrison then agreed to surrender but were tied back to back and thrown into the moat, and the castle was then mostly demolished. It is possible the keep was patched up and occupied for a while after this but it is shown as ruinous on the Buck print of 1731.

The castle has a low-lying site but originally probably had moats filled with water from the stream flowing past the east side which has cut into the supposed base of the NE tower. The Royalists justified killing the garrison in 1644 on the grounds that the Parliamentarians attempted to hold an indefensible site, since the moats and thin curtain wall offered little protection against the cannon of that period. The bailey was about 70m long and about 40m wide at the east end and 30m wide at the west end. What looks like a ramparted platform west of the keep set in the middle of the south side is actually the buried footings of three ranges of domestic buildings. To the south and west is a much larger outer bailey.

Hopton Castle

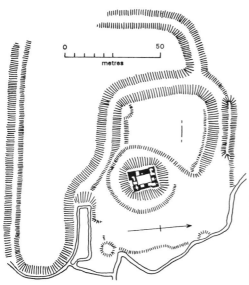

Site plan of Hopton Castle

Hopton Castle

The sandstone keep measured 13.7m by 11.7m above a battered plinth from which rise flat pilaster buttresses clasping the corners. There were two storeys, both living rooms with fireplaces in the north wall. The low gable with a small attic window set on the outer edge of the south wall is a Tudor addition and the original roof presumably lay within an embattled parapet. The entrance doorway lies at the north end at ground level and has a drawbar slot and a clear mark of the roof of the wooden porch burnt in the siege of 1644. Off the entrance passage leads a spiral stair in the NW corner. The lowest storey has four deep window embrasures off which lead small rooms each with two windows in the east corners and a latrine set in the more boldly projecting SW corner. The windows here are small, and one facing west is now only represented by a breach in the wall. The four upper windows were of two lights, at least one of them being a late medieval insertion. The room here is larger as the walls are reduced from their thickness below of 2.2m. Again there are square rooms in the eastern corners, presumably bedrooms, and in the SW corner was a suite of two rooms connected by a second spiral staircase in the west wall.

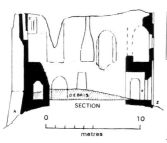

Plans and section of Hopton Castle

HUMPHRESTON HALL   SJ 818050

The existing hall is a half-timbered structure probably dating from the 17th century. Among the outbuildings is a stone structure of the same period with plain mullioned windows. The rectangle of water south of the hall is all that remains of the moat. Several iron cannon balls found within the grounds suggest an unrecorded siege during the Civil War. Not far west at SJ 814050 is an enclosure 33m long by 30m wide on a sloping site with a surrounding moat about 17m wide, now nearly dry. This may be that of the medieval hall of this district.

KINNERLEY CASTLE   SJ 341200

The castle of "Kinardsle" captured by Llywelyn ap Iorwerth in 1223 was probably the 4m high mound on flat ground by a stream at Belan Bank with traces of a crescent-shaped bailey platform 90m by 75m 1.5m high to the south. This may have been the castle of "Eggelawe" placed under the command of Robert de Vipont by King John in 1212, since a place called Edgerly lies nearby to the south. See photo page 88.

KNOCKIN CASTLE   SJ 336224

This castle was probably built by Guy Le Strange in the 1150s. Henry II had it repaired in 1165 and Richard I spent some money on it in 1196, but in 1198 it was returned to John Le Strange. In 1223 Henry III aided the rebuilding of the castle, presumably in stone. An inquisition on the death of Maud Le Strange in 1405 records the castle as occupied by Sir Nicholas Herbert. Knockin passed by marriage to the Stanley earls of Derby but the castle was probably then abandoned as Leland c1540 described it as a "ruinous thing". Stones from it were removed in 1818 to build a bridge and the present churchyard wall.

The earthworks comprise a quadrangular inner bailey 60m long by 40m wide, with an outer bailey, now occupied by the rectory, to the east. They lie between a pair of north-south flowing streams which probably provided water for wet moats. The inner bailey, now covered in trees, rises 3m above the surrounding ground. The rampart on the south and the mound on the east appear to cover the lower parts of a curtain wall. The outer bailey defences are mostly obliterated but on the south side, close to the inner bailey, is a rampart with the remains of a thick wall of sandstone blocks half buried in its inner side.

LANGLEY HALL   SJ 540002

Of the moated mansion of the Lee family there remains the gatehouse with a timber framed facade on the NE and an ashlar-faced facade on the SW towards the outside, with a double-chamfered entrance arch.

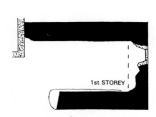
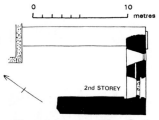
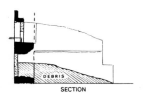

Plans and section of Lea Castle

Lea Castle

Lea Castle

LEA CASTLE   SO 352892

Adjoining a farmhouse of no great age, upon which is fixed a wooden shield dated 1560, are ruins of a 14th century tower, possibly built by Robert Corbet. He is recorded as living here in the 1320s, after the manor of Lydbury North, which also included Bishop's Castle 2.5km to the west, was confiscated from the Bishop of Hereford by Edward II. Although Bishop's Castle was later returned by Edward III to the bishop, Lea remained a Corbet residence until it was destroyed in October 1645 by Thomas Middleton. He "performed much gallant service" to the Parliamentary cause by sending a party of foot to Lea, which "took out" the Royalist garrison and sent them as prisoners to Redcastle. The tower is 9.4m wide over walls 2m thick and was over 15m long. The inserted window embrasure of 16th or 17th century in the south wall may be the arch revealed by excavation in 1844. The staircase visible in 1858 must have been in the north end wall, now entirely missing. At that time there were traces of the surrounding moat and a portcullis was "attached to the farmhouse". The portcullis evidently came from the upper doorway 4.5m above ground in the south end of the tower which has a groove for one, plus a drawbar for a door inside it. There is also one window loop at this end on the same level. East of this window is a row of four corbels carrying a slightly projecting section of walling. The portcullis must have been operated from a now destroyed third storey. The "north side wall which is of formidable strength" then partly remaining could have been part of a curtain wall, unless it referred to the tower.

Last remaining wall of Leigh Hall

Hopton Castle: entrance

LEIGH HALL   SJ 333037

Leigh Hall was a 14th century moated mansion like that at Cheney Longville, possibly built by the Hagars, who were originally tenants of the Corbets of Caus. The house was garrisoned by Sir Pelham Corbet in 1644 but was captured and burnt by Parliamentary forces in the spring of 1645. However, later drawings suggest it was repaired and occupied until the 18th century. The wet moat 7m wide is well preserved except on the south towards the existing farmhouse. Inside was a wall 1m thick enclosing a court 50m long by 25m wide. A small portion still stands 2m high on the south side next to where there was a projection. Buried footings suggest a range 11m wide externally on the NE where there is a causeway across the moat.

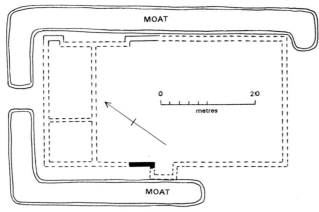

Plan of Leigh Hall

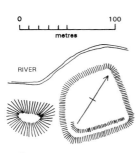

Little Shrawardine: plan

Gatehouse at Langley Hall

LITTLE SHRAWARDINE CASTLE SJ 393151

This site was probably the predecessor of the early 13th century stone castle on a weaker but more strategically useful site at Alberbury 3.5km to the west. The River Severn has washed away the northern half of a mound 9m high with a summit now measuring 15m by 5m. A track down to the river occupies the bottom of a ditch which separated the motte from a large quadrangular bailey to the NE.

LONGNOR: THE MOAT HOUSE SJ 494002

The present black and white house with closely spaced vertical timbers on both storeys was probably built for Edward Acton and Eleanor le Strange in the late 14th century. It held a Royalist garrison in 1645 and about that time an upper floor was inserted in the hall and a big stone chimney erected at the north end. Surrounding it is an irregularly shaped quadrangular moat which is crossed by three causeways and enclosed a platform 75m long by 50m wide. On the west side is the base of a gatehouse mentioned in the 1570s and probably like that at Stokesay. In the 1290s Richard and Emma Clerk were allowed by Roger Sprenchose (then lord of the manor of Longnor) to widen the moat externally by twelve feet. The "placea fossate" was sold by the then lord of the manor Gruffydd de le Pole to William Acton in 1310.

Motte at Little Shrawardine

LUDLOW CASTLE   SO 508746

Ludlow has one of the finest medieval castles in Britain. Although the roofs and floors are missing from the keep and apartments in the inner bailey most of the stonework remains almost complete and comparatively free of 18th, 19th and 20th century repairs and alterations. The castle was a rarity in 11th century England in being stone walled from the beginning and it remained a major stronghold and administrative centre until abandoned in the 1680s, at all periods eclipsing all the other castles in Shropshire. At the time of the Domesday Book survey of 1086 this district was part of the large manor of Stanton Lacy then held by Roger de Lacy, who had recently succeeded his father Walter. It is generally assumed that the castle was built by Roger between 1086 and 1095, when he quarrelled with William II and fled into exile, probably leaving the building stilll incomplete. Henry I is said to have granted Ludlow to Joce de Dinan. The castle is first mentioned in 1139 when King Stephen unsuccessfully besieged it. The mound removed in the 1190s for extensions to the parish church may have been a siege-work of that period, possibly adapted from a barrow. There was a dramatic episode during the siege when the king in person rescued the teenage Prince Henry of Scotland who was seized by a grappling hook thrown out from the castle walls. Joce de Dinan is said to have later ambushed and captured his unruly neighbour Hugh de Mortimer, a supporter of King Stephen, and held him prisoner in the keep until a large ransom was paid.

The de Lacys are thought to have added the outer bailey during the early part of Henry II's reign. Their success in Ireland caused friction with the Crown and Ludlow was held by Henry II during the 1180s, royal expenditure on it being recorded, and King John was in possession from 1213 until his death in 1216. It was then recovered by Walter de Lacy. In 1225 Henry III signed a peace treaty with Llywelyn ap Iorwerth at Ludlow and about that time the castle was given by the king to William Gamages, whilst in 1232 the king issued a patent for walling the town. On the death of Walter de Lacy in 1241 Ludlow passed by marriage to the Grenvilles. Two Grenville heiresses married Roger Mortimer of Wigmore and Theobald de Verdon of Alton. The two lords shared the castle and this is thought to be the reason why the fine 14th century hall has splendid apartments at both ends. Roger Mortimer became sole owner in 1316. He governed England from 1326 along with his lover Queen Isabella, after they deposed Edward II, but was executed when the teenage Edward III took control of his own affairs in 1330.

In 1424 Ludlow passed by marriage to Richard, Earl of Cambridge, who became Duke of York in 1426. Henry VI advanced with a large Lancastrian army towards Ludlow in 1459, where the Duke and his allies had mustered the Yorkist forces. At a critical moment Sir Andrew Wallop, Marshal of the Yorkist army, deserted to the Lancastrians. Thus weakened the Yorkists fled leaving the castle to be "robbed to the bare walls" by the Lancastrians. Duke Richard was killed in battle at Wakefield in 1460 but in 1461 his son won battles at Mortimer's Cross and Barnet and took the throne as Edward IV. In 1472 Edward set up the Council of the Welsh Marches with Bishop Alcock as first president and Ludlow Castle as its base. The keep was then remodelled and a new block of apartments built in the inner ward. Edward's infant sons Edward and Richard were sent to Ludlow to act as figureheads under the guardianship of the Queen Elizabeth's brother Lord Rivers. On Edward IV's death in 1483 the two young princes were sent to the Tower of London, where they mysteriously disappeared and their uncle took the throne as Richard III. Henry VII followed Edward IV's example and sent his eldest son Arthur to live at Ludlow, but the prince died there in 1502, not long after his unconsummated marriage to Catherine of Aragon, later the first wife of his younger brother, Henry VIII.

Mortimer's Tower

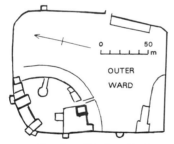

Site plan of Ludlow Castle

The keep of Ludlow Castle

Elizabeth I appointed Sir Henry Sidney as Lord President of the Council of the Marches in 1559, a post he held until he died at the castle in 1586. He was active in the affairs of the town, and erected various buildings at the castle, notably the judges' lodgings by the entrance to the inner ward. The Earl of Pembroke was then President until 1601, then Lord Zouche, and from 1631 onwards Sir John Egerton, later created Earl of Bridgwater. Soon afterwards he entertained at Ludlow King Charles, who had made a previous visit in 1616, and the castle hall was the scene of the first production of the famous play "The Masque of Comus" by Milton, inspired by an incident in which the earl's son and daughter got lost in Hayward Forest. Ludlow was the last Shropshire castle to hold out for King Charles, only surrendering on the 1st of June 1646. Under Charles II his cousin Prince Rupert was Lord President, Rupert having commanded the castle in 1645, and the castle having survived the Civil War without being slighted because it was needed as an administrative centre. It was still in use as a prison in 1688 but in 1689 William III abolished the office of Lord President and the castle was left to decay. It was purchased by the Earl of Powys in 1811 and remains part of that estate.

Keep doorway at Ludlow

Hall at Ludlow

The late 11th century defences of the inner ward survive in a remarkably complete state. On the east side and south sides, towards the later outer ward, the 2.4m thick curtain wall curves round and has in front of it a rock-cut ditch 13m wide. The other sides stand above steep rocky slopes and were flanked by four square towers, the northern two of which have their angles chamfered off. These two were heightened by one extra storey when the fine set of apartments were laid out between them in the early 14th century. Except for the small tower on the west side with a north-facing postern in its base, the towers were open to the court at ground level, but there were rooms above with their inner walls set on arches.

The 11th century gatehouse was a long T-shaped tower with two wings carried up as turrets. These turrets contain original windows and gave the southern aspect of the building an impressiveness out of proportion to its real width. A timber bridge over the ditch led into a high porch 4m deep and then through a pair of strong doors into a long, high passage with three machicolation slots in the vault and having another set of doorway at the far end. The outer doorways were opened onto for carts and important personages for there was a narrow and easier to defend side-passage for pedestrians. Both sides of the main passage had four bays of blind arcading but little now remains of this. Above the passage there was originally just a hall reached by a straight stair in the thickness of the east wall rising to a lobby in the east turret. The walls then rose up high above the room to protect its roof.

Sometime during the mid or late 12th century the gatehouse was converted into a keep by blocking the entrance passage to create a cellar and widening the building by erecting a groin-vaulted bedroom with a latrine behind the west turret. The bedroom has two original windows, plus a much larger wooden framed one of the 17th century. In the 1470s the north end of the keep was rebuilt shorter than before. The stair to the hall was blocked and replaced by a spiral stair with a fine new ornamental doorway facing towards the entrance passage into the inner ward created east of the keep. By lowering the hall ceiling and using the space in the roof it was possible to create two extra upper chambers, whilst the cellar was divided by a floor into two levels, so that there were now five storeys in all, thus creating a tower house comparable to others built by leading Yorkists in this period at Ashby-de-la-Zouch and Raglan.

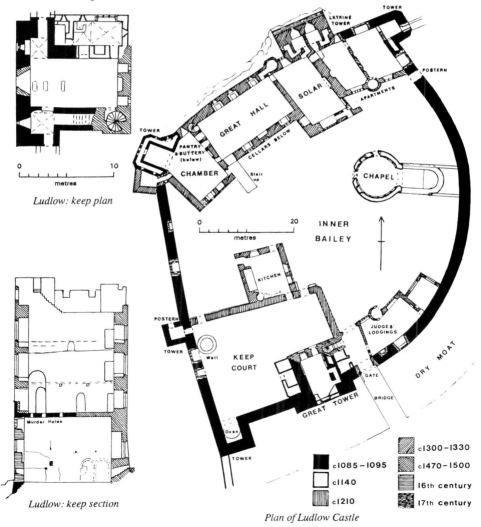

Ludlow: keep plan

Ludlow: keep section

Plan of Ludlow Castle

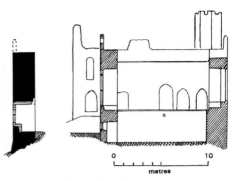

Ludlow: sections of curtain wall and great hall

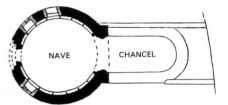

Chapel doorway at Ludlow

Ludlow: plan of chapel

A stone bridge over the dry ditch leads to the 14th century entrance arch of the inner ward which was closed merely with a two-leaved door. The passage then leads through the lowest storey of the range of apartments erected by Sir Henry Sidney to accommodate the itinerant judges serving the Marches. Above the gateway is a plaque with his arms and those of Elizabeth I, England and France, with the date Anno Regni Regina Elizabeth 23 (1581). The irregularly shaped range has high gables in place of the original parapet of the curtain wall, through which are pieced deep embrasures for mullion and transom windows.

The whole north side of the bailey is occupied by palatial early 14th century domestic buildings. A wide stair opposite the kitchen leads up to the great hall, raised above a cellar. There are three windows with seats in the embrasures on each side. One of those facing the court, which are of two lights, was later blocked when a fireplace was inserted to replace the original central fire on a stone base in the centre of the floor. The hall doorway still has its original door and gives only a passage which was screened off from the main hall to exclude draughts. Service doorways off the passage led to stairs down to a buttery and pantry in the basement of the wing to the west. The upper two storeys of the wing were reached from a now-destroyed porch in front of the hall doorway and were pleasant living rooms of considerable size with bedrooms in the older adjacent NW tower. Doorways at the dais end of the hall lead onto another spiral stair and into the lower of two large chambers with fine fireplaces set above a basement in the east solar block. Adjoining the block is a 14th century tower containing latrines and small chambers, and beyond is a range which has north facing windows of the 1470s, although the south wall with a spiral staircase turret adjoining the spine wall is of the late 16th century.

The apartments at Ludlow Castle

One of the rarest and most interesting features of the castle is the round naved chapel built c1140. Only four other round medieval naves remain in Britain, all built in imitation of Holy Sepulchre church at Jerusalem built c1099. Foundations are all that remain of the original polygonal apsed chancel and its timber framed 16th century successor which extended further to meet the curtain wall. The nave has blank arcading inside, and a west doorway and chancel with much zig-zag or chevron ornament in the arches. The doorway has ornamented scallop capitals and there are three original nook-shafted windows. Two lower windows were inserted in the 16th century, when the nave was given an upper floor which was connected to the eastern solar block by a timber framed gallery, creating a small private court to the north. South of the chancel are traces of a timber building marked as a laundry on an old plan made for the Earl of Powys.

Distant view of Ludlow

Keep and Judges' Lodgings at Ludlow

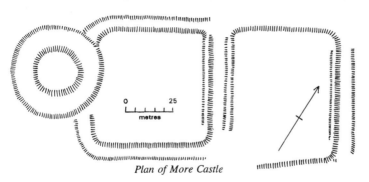

Plan of More Castle

The large outer ward provided space for stables, stores and workshops. It was built upon space formerly occupied by part of the early 12th century town, resulting in the west end of the High Street being cut off. The outer gateway may have once been more imposing than at present. By the curtain to the south are the porter's lodgings, prison and stables built by Sir Henry Sidney and now restored from ruin to provide an office and shop for the custodian. North of the gateway is a late 12th century rectangular tower of four storeys backing onto the still-inhabited buildings in the northern part of the ward, which is closed off from the public. High above the river on the west side is the D-shaped Mortimer's Tower of c1300-20 with shouldered-lintelled doorways leading out onto the curtain wall-walk. The basement was a vaulted gateway passage with a portcullis in the outer arch until both ends were blocked in the 16th century. It seems strange that this difficult to reach gateway should have a portcullis yet neither of the inner nor outer main gates ever had one. On the south side of the outer ward, now accessible from outside, is a chapel of St Peter built in the 1320s but extended westwards when converted into a courthouse in the 16th century. North of it was the 16th century "Tennys Corte".

Substantial portions of the 13th century town wall lie hidden away behind houses and gardens. On the south side is Broad Gate, still inhabited, and a sort of misnomer for although it has twin flanking D-shaped towers, the passageway, closed by a portcullis and a pair of doors, was rather narrow for a town gateway of this type.

Broad Gate, Ludlow Town Wall

LYDHAM CASTLE   SO 334910

West of the church is a D-shaped bailey platform with a ditch on the north side. The nearly straight west side is about 60m long and has a motte in the middle rising barely 3m above the bailey but rather more above the stream to the west.

MEOLE BRACE TOWER   SJ 487105

An inquisition of 1273, on the death of George, 4th and last Baron Cantilupe of Abergavenny, refers to a "fortified dwelling called a tower and other poor buildings". The manor had passed to the Cantilupes c1211 from the de Bracey family. It passed to the Zouche family and in 1490 was occupied by Thomas Mackworth, who was married to a cousin of Lord Zouche. In 1537 Lord Zouche bequeathed the tower to Arthur Mackworth, whose descendants sold the "manor house or capital messuage called the castle" to Thomas Edwards. It was accidentally destroyed by fire some time during Charles II's reign and nothing now remains of it, the site being on the west bank of the Rea Brook, near the church, 2km south of Shrewsbury.

MORE CASTLE   SO 339914

In the field west of More church is a mound rising 2.5m above a ditch 9m wide to a summit 25m across, whilst to the east is an inner bailey 58m square and beyond it an outer bailey 50m by 85. Excavation of the motte in 1959 found pieces of 12th and 13th century pottery and showed it had been created by filling in the centre of a ringwork. This may possibly be the otherwise unidentified Matefelun (thought to have been in this area) where William de Botterell was licensed to fortify his house in 1195, the work being subsidised by a grant of 10 marks from Richard I..

The keep, Moreton Corbet

Moreton Corbet: the Elizabethan mansion

MORETON CORBET CASTLE   SJ 561231   E

As late as 1516 Moreton Corbet was still known as Moreton Toret (or Turret) after the Toret family. The keep was probably built by Bartholomew Fitz Toret but was taken from him by King John in 1215. Henry III handed it back in 1217, but in the 1230s it passed by marriage to the Corbet family. Leland mentions "a fair castle of Mr Corbettes" here c1540. The long Elizabethan mansion on the south side was begun in the 1560s by Sir Andrew Corbet and has on the SW the year 1579 (when he died) and the cypher E.R. (Elizabeth Regina). The work was still not completed when his son Robert died in 1583. The postern in the curtain wall just north of the keep and several windows through the curtain wall were hastily blocked up in 1644 when the castle was garrisoned by the Royalists. Parliamentary troops captured the castle in September of that year and burnt it when they left in March 1645. The site was afterwards sold by Sir Vincent Corbet and probably never reoccupied. Andrew Corbet purchased the ruin back in 1743. Since 1949 it has been in state care as an ancient monument, the custodians now being English Heritage.

The NW wall and the adjacent part of the NE wall of the keep stand to the full height except the battlements but only foundation remain of the rest, probably the result of slighting in 1645. Above a broad battered plinth from which rise corner pilaster buttresses it measured 12m by 9.1m over walls 1.7m thick. There were three storeys but the topmost level was probably formed later out of what was originally roof space. The storage basement had a loop in each wall. The hall above was larger because of a reduction in the wall thickness and has remains of a fine fireplace with polygonal shafts carrying capitals with upright leaves. Beside it a doorway was later inserted to give access to other rooms added beyond.

Keep at Moreton Corbet

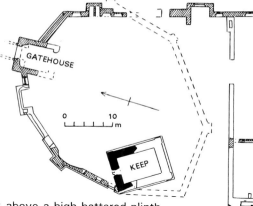

Plan of Moreton Corbet Castle

The bailey wall is 1.3m thick above a high battered plinth and originally probably rose directly from the water of a moat up to 12m wide. On the NW corner is a small rectangular turret. The fireplace behind the turret, the two small loops, the postern doorway with an only slightly pointed head and the roof mark on the keep north wall are relics of a two storey range built here in the early 16th century. A roof mark indicates another building lay east of the keep. The gatehouse bears the date 1579 with the initials R.A.C. and the Corbets' elephant and castle crest and was evidently remodelled in that year, although the basic shell of the building including the portcullis groove is more likely to be 14th century work. On the outer face are traces of the side parapets of a bridge over the moat. West of the gatehouse is an early Tudor window of two lights with four-centred heads, whilst to the east is a stretch of 13th century curtain wall later rebuilt on the old base. On the east side of the bailey is the outer wall of an early 16th century range of at least two storeys. There are several blocked three-light windows and projections containing pairs of latrines and fireplaces set one above another.

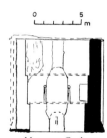

Moreton Corbet: section of keep

Moreton Corbet Castle from the north

The gatehouse at Moreton Corbet   *East side of Moreton Corbet Castle*

The Elizabethan mansion probably lies south of where the medieval great hall was and perhaps incorporates some of its materials. It is 52m long by 9.8m wide and built of brick and sadstone but faced on the outside with fine grey ashlar. The north front containing the entrance is mostly destroyed and the south front is far from complete but enough survives to make a splendid ruin, even if the internal layout is difficult to reconstruct. There were two lofty storeys of fine apartments plus attics and basements below each end. The south front has three slightly projecting bays containing five-light mullion-and-transom windows, and there were columns and three-light windows in between. The lower columns are Tuscan and the upper columns are Ionic, and dividing the two main storeys is an ornamented metope frieze. Above the bays were ogival gables with attic windows, giving a well indented skyline. Inside there were nearly square rooms at either end and two rectangular state rooms in the middle in each storey. Fireplaces were provided in the crosswalls and there are latrine pits by the western crosswall and at the NE corner. The north facade is known from old illustrations to have had a central seven-light window on each main storey and a segmental pediment. There were four-light windows on either side with normal pediments and ogival gables as on the south side.

The Elizabethan mansion at Moreton Corbet

MYDDLE CASTLE   SJ 468237

John Le Strange of Knockin was licensed by Edward II to crenellate his manor house of "Medle" in 1308. It passed by marriage c1450 to the Kynastons, one of whom, "Wild Humphry" was outlawed for a murder committed in Church stretton in 1491 and lived a Robin Hood style of live based on a cave on the side of Nesscliffe Hill until his death in 1534. The castle passed to the Stanley earls of Derby and was described c1540 by Leland as "veri ruinus". Myddle was later sold to the Egertons but the castle was never used by them. It was a modest rectangular courtyard house with a wet moat still full of water a century ago but now filled in. On the south side is the base of a wall 1.8m thick. The only other remains are slight traces of the footing of a thin internal wall on the NE and the stump of a stair turret forming the NW corner of the inner court. More stood of this turret until 1970. It has a doorway with a wide cusped head from the west range, which was the hall, and adjacent to the south is one jamb of a lofty transomed window of 14th century type looking east. The stair was the means of access from the dais end of the wall to private rooms set on two storeys of the north range. By the doorway is a stone recording repairs to the turret in 1649 by the Rt Hon John Hume Egerton, Viscount Alford. A description of the castle by Gough in his "History of Myddle" suggests that there was an outer court with its own gatehouse and moat to the east, and that the kitchen lay in the east range south of the inner gatehouse, and there were further apartments in the south range. He also mentions a flat roof reached by the staircase in the turret and that there was another staircase in the SW corner of the inner court.

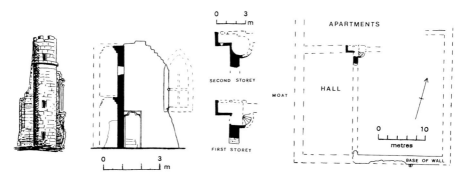

Plans, section and view of Myddle Castle before collapse

Myddle Castle

OSWESTRY CASTLE   SJ 292298   F

The castle at Oswestry belonging to Rainald the Bailleul, Sheriff of Shropshire, is one of the few castles in Shropshire mentioned in the Domesday Book survey of 1086. It was probably founded several years earlier by his predecessor as sheriff, Warin the Bald, who died in 1085. Rainald was succeeded in 1098 by his step-son Hugh Fitz-Warine, but Oswestry later passed to Alan Fitz-Flaald, a descendant of Rainald's wife. In 1148 the castle was captured from his son William Fitz-Alan by Madoc ap Meredith, but it was later recovered by William. In the 1160s a new well was dug and palisades provided, but if the sum of money allegedly spent on the castle during that period (£2,000) is correct then the work must have included the building of a stone keep and bailey wall. In 1212 King John took the castle from John Fitz-Alan, placing it firstly in the care of Robert de Vipont, then John Marshal, and finally Thomas de Erdington, but in 1214 John Fitza-Alan recaptured the castle. King John burnt the town in 1216 but failed to capture the castle. The town was burnt again in 1263, this time by Prince Llywelyn. At the start of his operations against the Welsh Prince in 1277 Edward I ordered the town to be enclosed with a stone wall but this failed to save it from another burning in the early 1400s by Owain Glyndwr. A survey of the castle after the execution of Richard Fitz-Alan, Earl of Arundel in 1397 mentions the great, middle and high chambers the wardrobe, the constable's hall, the buttery, the chapel, the kitchen and the larder. In 1398 Richard II adjourned a Parliament from Shrewsbury to Oswestry and there ordered the Dukes of Norfolk and Hereford to fight a duel at Coventry to settle their quarrel.

In 1603 the castle was granted to Thomas Howard, Earl of Suffolk, but was sold by him to Dame Elizabeth Craven, from whom it descended to the earls of Powys. It was garrisoned for King Charles in 1643, and captured by Parliamentary forces in 1644. It was destroyed in 1647, except that some buildings seem to have been spared either as a residence or for administrative purposes.

All that now remains of the castle is a 9m high mound in a public park. The summit (reached by a spiral path) commands extensive views and is a quadrangle about 28m by 17m. On the SE side are two fragments of masonry, one in situ, the other fallen. Old drawings show the keep as being low and quadrangular and the remains seem to bear this out, but it is not possible to say whether the structure was an open court or wholly roofed over. The fallen fragment indicates a wall thickness of 2m. The bailey south of the mound is now absorbed by the town and built over. The line of the bailey defences can be traced in the horseshoe shape made by Leg St, Cross St and Willow St. Leland only mentions the buildings on the mound so the town may already have encroached on the bailey by the 1530s.

The town walls begun in 1277 had an average thickness of 2.1m. The line of the defences can be traced on the west side, where there is a road called Welsh Walls. Any remaining fragments are hidden away amongst buildings and gardens. Of the four town gateways the Black Gate was demolished in 1771, and New Gate, Willow Gate and Beatrice Gate were destroyed in 1782.

PLAISH HALL   SO 530964

The H-shaped brick mansion built c1540 by Sir William Leighton has three and four light windows with arched lights. One room has panels painted with initials of Henry VIII. The house incorporates at the SW end stonework of an older house with one three-light 15th century window. A house existed here by 1255 and the moat which could still be traced as late as 1868 may have gone back to that period.

The last remains of the keep on the motte at Oswestry

PONTESBURY CASTLE   SJ 401058

A mound 3.5m high and 45m across to the NE of the church was excavated in 1961-4 before a housing estate was built over it. Along with 12th and 13th century pottery were found massive foundations of a tower keep of c1200 estimated as being about 18m square. The castle was a Corbet possession until c1300, when, on the excavation evidence, it was burnt and not reoccupied. A document of 1353 suggests there were then no buildings but c1540 Leland saw "great tokens of stones fallen down of a great manor place or castle", and sandstone walling was visible on the site until robbed in the 19th century.

QUATFORD CASTLE   SO 738908   F

The castle, church (formerly collegiate) and borough of Quatford were all established in the 1070s by Roger de Montgomery, allegedly in fulfilment of a vow made by his second wife Adeliza, when she was in danger of shipwreck in the English Channel, to found a church at the spot where she first met the earl. Overlooking the site of an ancient ford across the River Severn is a ridge of sandstone which ends in a vertical cliff above the river. On the top is a small but steeply sided motte rising 7m above a rock-cut ditch which separates it from a kidney shaped bailey to the east. The bailey was commanded by the churchyard further east and it was undoubtedly this weakness that prompted Roger's son Robert de Bellesme to transfer the whole settlement in 1101 to the larger and stronger site 3km upstream at Bridgnorth. Excavations carried out on the east side of the bailey in 1960 prior to the widening of the main road cutting through the ridge, found many post holes for timber building, but no sign of a ditch.

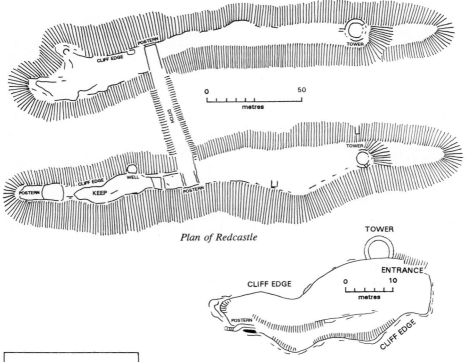

Plan of Redcastle

Plan of the keep or citadel of Redcastle

Redcastle: well tower

RED CASTLE   SJ 572296 & 564292

In 1228 Henry III licensed Henry de Audley to construct the castle of Redcliffe, later known as Red Castle. Little now remains of it, but the site is spectacular and the layout large and unusual with some affinities with the castle of the Earl of Chester at Beeston in Cheshire, begun c1220, and the slightly later royal castles of Montgomery and Deganwy in Wales. It presumably replaced an earlier wooden castle of the mound rising 5m to a 15m diameter summit on a hill north of the church. In 1283 Red Castle was reported to be in good repair but had an "insufficient garrison". Whatever its merits as a fortification, Red Castle was not very suitable for purely residential use and the place seems to have been abandoned after the death of James, Lord Audley in 1386. The site was purchased by Henry VIII in 1536 and around that time was described by Leland as "now all ruinous", although it is said to have held a Parliamentary garrison in 1645. Elizabeth I granted Red Castle to Sir Andrew Corbet and in the 18th century it was acquired by the Hills.

The castle was roughly a rectangle of 160m by 90m and lay on and between two narrow craggy sandstone ridges forming the east and west lines of defence. Between them is a wooded valley about 9m deep on the south and as much as 20m deep on the north, where the ridges rise as sheer cliffs. A ditch 3m deep traverses this valley near the middle of its length and is continued into the ridges as man-made chasms, just enough native rock being left on the outer sides to carry the main outer wall. Posterns are contrived through the rock leading from the chasms to the outside, that on the west being a winding tunnel of considerable length. Nothing now remains of the former curtain walls which closed off the valley north and south ends. On the ridges the soft sandstone was quarried into walls and chambers where possible and the masonry walls and towers were provided only where really necessary, and not built to any great height. Much of the circuit of the walls was no more than a high parapet 0.6m thick set on the cliff edge. Most of it has crumbled away with the natural rock, and only a small fragment towards the south end of the west side remains standing. At the south end of each ridge are the footings of round towers about 9m in diameter over walls 2m thick. Further north on the east ridge is a curved face in the natural rock with holes for floor beams of a tower of which no actual masonry walls now survive. The two projecting crags at the northern end of the east ridge both bore turrets but only the eastern one now remains. It measures 3.7m in diameter over walling 0.6m thick.

The northern half of the western ridge is divided into two by a second chasm and there are remains of a polygonal bastion on the small piece of ridge between the two cuttings. The remainder of the north end of the ridge is the highest and least accessible part of the whole site. It evidently formed an unusual type of citadel or keep in the form of an irregularly shaped area 43m long with a parapet around the cliff edge. There are no remains of any interior structures and only a small defaced fragment of the wall remains at the north end next to a rock-cut postern leading out to some steps down to an outwork immediately below the keep. At the south end of the east side is a tower which extends all the way down to the valley about 16m below to enclose a well shaft extending a further 15m down into the rock. A postern allowed the well to be reached from the bailey. The tower is built of sandstone blocks with a chamfered plinth and contained several rooms communicating with each other only by trap doors and ladders. Although sometimes claimed as a folly built by the Hills in the 1780s, everything below the former top storey shown on old pictures appears to be original medieval work, complete with arrow-slits.

Ruyton Castle

ROWTON CASTLE   SJ 379128

The existing castle is an impressive castellated building resulting from additions of 1809-12 and c1824-8 by Colonel Henry Lyster to a brick house erected on or near the site of the old castle under the terms of the will of Richard Lyster dated 1696. A castle here is first mentioned in 1282, when it was destroyed by the Welsh. It belonged either to the Corbets or the Le Stranges but subsequently, having been rebuilt, passed to the Lovells, and then to the Lysters in the 1460s. The story of Lady Lyster surrendering the castle on honourable terms after a siege by Parliamentary forces in 1645 appears to be a 19th century fabrication. The truth appears to be that the Royalists simply abandoned the castle and one side or the other burnt it.

RUYTON CASTLE   SJ 393223   F

Three defaced fragments of a keep about 14m square over walls 3m thick lie immediately west of the parish church, which stands on a fairly steep sided low promontory south of the River Parry. The only remaining features are two shafts in the south wall and part of a third on the north. The Le Stranges are said to have abandoned the castle in favour of that at Knockin and it was ruinous in 1272, having been damaged by Fulke Fitz Warine in 1203 and by the Welsh in 1212. In the early 14th century the castle was sold by John Le Strange to Edmund, Earl of Arundel, by whom it was rebuilt, although he can hardly have been a frequent visitor. In the 1320s Ruyton was held by Roger Mortimer, Earl of March, but after his execution in 1330 by Edward III it reverted to the Earl of Arundel. It seems to have been abandoned in the 1360s and was plundered for materials to build the west tower of the church. For many years there was a cottage built into the ruin of the keep. The castle area became part of the graveyard c1880.

SHERIFFHALES CASTLE   SJ 756121

The half-timbered manor house west of the church stands near a pool which may be a relic of a moat. This is probably the site of the manor house which William Trussell of Cubleston was licensed to crenellate by Edward III in 1367.

Shrawardine Castle

SHRAWARDINE CASTLE   SJ 401184

Domesday Book in 1086 records the manor of Shrawardine as held by Rainald de Bailleul. Sheriff of Shropshire, and he probably built a castle here. It is first mentioned in 1165 when Philip Helgot acknowledged that he owed service of "castle guard-the same as his antecessors had been used to render". Henry II sent nearly £20 on repairs to the castle in 1171-2 and it was well maintained by the crown as an outpost of Shrewsbury until destroyed by the Welsh in 1215. The surviving masonry probably dates when the 1220s. Henry III declined to bear the cost of rebuilding the castle himself but ordered his officials to make materials available to John Fitz-Alan, who was given custody. His descendants remained in possession until the castle was sold in 1583 to Sir Thomas Bromley, Lord High Chancellor. His son Sir Henry made the castle his principal residence and improved the accommodation. It was garrisoned for King Charles in 1643, and in September 1644 Sir William Vaughan, the commander, destroyed most of the church, the parsonage and the castle outbuildings to give the garrison a clear field of fire. After a five day siege in June 1645, during which the rest of the village was destroyed, the castle was surrendered and it was then dismantled by Parliamentary forces, the timberwork being burnt and the stones taken off to Shrewsbury to repair the defences there.

The castle lies on a gentle rise east of the River Severn. It consists of a low mound or ringwork with the last remnants of a retaining shell wall rising from the bottom of the ditch. On the west are remains of an ashlar plinth with relieving arches and a keeled roll moulding at the junction with the vertical wall, of which there remain just two small defaced fragments rising out 6m above the ditch. On the north and east the exact line of the wall is unclear, but there are traces of its base on the south. The third standing fragment and a nearby curved base appear to be relics of a gateway flanked by twin drum towers, as at the contemporary inner ward at Whittington. There may well have been several other such towers. Traces remain of the internal buildings on the west side and the uneven ground within the court covers the foundations of several others. There are slight traces of a U-shaped bailey platform 38m across each way to the SE.

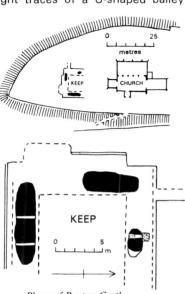

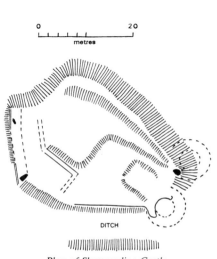

Plan of Shrawardine Castle

Plans of Ruyton Castle

SHREWSBURY CASTLE   SJ 388206   O

Shrewsbury is almost entirely surrounded by a loop of the River Severn and in 1067 William I ordered a castle constructed beside the vulnerable neck of land on the north. In 1069 "the Welsh, with the men of Cheshire, laid siege to the King's castle of Shrewsbury aided by the townsmen under Edric the Wild". The castle held out although the town was burnt as a relieving force got near. In 1074 William I gave the castle to his kinsman Roger de Montgomery, created Earl of Shrewsbury. Domesday Book records the recent destruction of 51 houses for an extension to the castle, undoubtedly the outer bailey, and a similar number were destroyed to give a clear field of fire round the defences. The castle reverted to the crown when Robert de Bellesme's castles were surrendered to Henry I in 1102. William Fitz-Alan of Oswestry later had custody of the castle. He fortified it for the late King Henry I's daughter Matilda in defiance of the new king, Stephen. In 1139 King Stephen stormed the castle, summarily hanging nearly a hundred of the garrison.

The early castle defences were of earth and wood, the oldest stone parts dating from when the castle became royal again under Henry II. The Pipe Rolls record minor expenditure upon it in the 1160s and later. A shell keep was built on the mound summit and a modest curtain wall built around the inner bailey. Excavations have shown that the now-destroyed outer bailey wall had open backed square towers like those at Henry II's other castles at Dover and Orford. Llywelyn ap Iorweth captured both the town and castle in 1215, and this prompted work to be started on a town wall in 1218 on the orders of the young Henry III. This work also included walling the east or river side of the outer bailey. Llywelyn attacked Shrewsbury again in 1234 and the walls were only finally completed in 1242, when the Dominican friars were given 200 cartloads of stone that were left over.

The main gateway at Shrewsbury

The mound summit and Laura's Tower at Shrewsbury

The great wooden tower which collapsed c1270 must have been inside the shell wall on the motte. River erosion caused the east side of the mound to subside, taking half the summit with it. This necessitated building a new retaining wall on this side, giving the present summit enclosure an odd shape. Edward I in c1288 had the hall block rebuilt and added the two round towers on the outer corners. The castle was neglected for three centuries, being "utterly wasted" in the 1420s and "muche in ruine" when visited by Leland, whilst more of the motte had collapsed in 1443.

Elizabeth I leased the castle to Richard Onslow and the former roof space then became the bedrooms of what had become his town house. It was later leased to the bailiffs and burgesses of the town. When Charles I came to Shrewsbury in 1642 the castle was too decayed to offer accommodation to the king and his officers, but in 1643 Lord Capel, newly appointed Lieutenant General of Shropshire, Cheshire and North Wales, set about repairing and improving the defences of both town and castle. The postern gateway was rebuilt, whilst the inner bailey main gateway was provided with a new iron-studded gate, still in position, and a barbican with musket loops. Prince Rupert was in command here in 1644 before going north to Marston Moor. The town was captured in a night attack early in 1645 after the Parliamentary forces under Colonel Reinking discovered a weakness in the defences. The castle was surrendered a few hours later on terms allowing the garrison to go to Ludlow. Parliament retained a garrison in the castle throughout the Commonwealth period and although there were plots by local Royalists to seize it they came to nothing.

The castle was handed over by the corporation to Charles II in 1663 and was then granted to Sir Francis Newport. It was subsequently leased to various families until it was acquired by Sir William Pulteney in the late 18th century. He commissioned Thomas Telford to restore the hall block as a residence and the little octagonal folly or gazebo built on the mound was named Laura's Tower after Sir William's daughter. The castle was acquired by Shropshire Horticultural Society in 1924 and presented to the Corporation, who used the hall block for council meetings until the 1980s. It is now a regimental museum and the inner bailey grounds are open to the public.

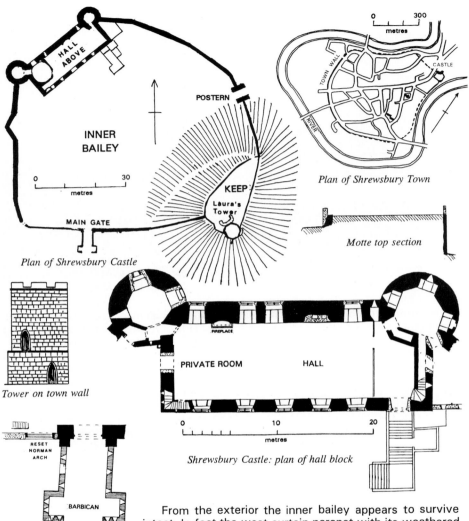

HALL ABOVE

INNER BAILEY

POSTERN

0   30
metres

MAIN GATE

KEEP

Laura's Tower

Plan of Shrewsbury Castle

0   300
metres

TOWN WALL

RIVER

CASTLE

Plan of Shrewsbury Town

Motte top section

Tower on town wall

RESET NORMAN ARCH

BARBICAN

Plan of gateway

FIREPLACE

PRIVATE ROOM   HALL

0   10   20
metres

Shrewsbury Castle: plan of hall block

Section through hall block

From the exterior the inner bailey appears to survive intact. In fact the west curtain parapet with its weathered cross-loops is probably of the Civil War period, and the other wall tops, parapets and roofs, plus many of the other details, are of the 18th and 19th centuries. There were once many buildings scattered around within the bailey, but, apart from the hall, we know only of the chapel of St Michael near to the mound. It was ruinous by 1395 and in 1605 the Corporation ordered an enquiry into how much stone was being taken from it, presumably by unauthorised persons. The outer bailey may have been reclaimed by the town by Elizabeth I's reign and all that remains of its defences is a short section of walling 2m thick by the river, pierced by the 13th century St Mary's Water gate.

The inner bailey is entered by a 12th century archway 2.7m wide set in a wall 1.5m thick. There are no traces of a tower, although one is shown projecting internally here on a plan of 1627. The gateway was closed simply by a two-leaved door. There was presumably once a ditch crossed by a drawbridge in front, where there is now a 17th century barbican, the innermost portion of which seems to have been roofed over to form a porch. Reset in the 19th century walling immediately to the west is a second Norman arch of c1200 with slightly finer mouldings. This was probably the chancel arch of the chapel of St Nicholas which stood in the outer bailey on or near the site of the present Presbyterian church, which survived until the mid 19th century. The doorway with a wooden lintel at the SW corner is 16th or 17th century. The west curtain wall has a curious salient angle projecting out. This does not seem medieval so a 17th century date is more likely, although it would make more military sense if it were further south.

All the castle buildings are faced with blocks of a type of sandstone which crumbles easily, hence considerable rebuilding over the years. The only masonry which looks different is the rough rubble section containing the gateway which is probably all that survives from Henry II's bailey walls. The remainder is perhaps a rebuild after the Welsh attack of 1215. The walls are not very thick or high and the thin sections on either side of the postern gate have no wall-walk. The postern gate measures 6.1m by 4.4m externally and has a single room with plain mullioned windows and plain battlements over a gateway passage 2.2m wide. The upper parts are 17th century but the passage with a portcullis groove and door rebates must be 13th century work. It seems odd that the main gateway never had a portcullis.

The hall block at Shrewsbury

The hall block at Shrewsbury

Of the 12th century shell keep there survive only the footings of a wall about 1.2m thick below the much later parapet facing the bailey. On the east is a retaining wall built in the 13th century to support what remained after the collapse of the motte top, but again the parapet is not old. Standing over the base of a small original round turret is a two storey gazebo of the 1790s with curved exterior stairs. The 1627 plan shows a round tower on this side of the mound summit but it is difficult to believe that a mound known to be prone to collapse has ever supported anything larger or more massive than the present folly tower of quite modest size.

No Norman features remain in the hall block so it can be regarded as essentially of the 1280s with later additions. In the much altered lowest storey are a 16th century fireplace and a circular 18th century office. Only the unlit circular room 3.3m in diameter in the base of the eastern tower remains in its 13th century state. This level once contained stores and a kitchen unless there was one in a separate detached building. The upper storey now forms one long chamber but originally the western third was divided off from the hall in the remaining part by a timber framed wall to form a private room with a central north fireplace flanked on each side by a deep embrasure with seats for a two-light window with Y-tracery. The west tower contained two polygonal bedrooms and also had a private back entrance to the royal suite at this end. From the solar stairs in the west and south walls led up to top room in the tower and down to the wine cellar below. The hall has three south windows and two on the north which were set on either side of a now-removed fireplace. In the late 16th century a new roof of low pitch was added higher up and the old roof space was used to create a low top storey with mullion-and-transom windows inserted on the south side.

There are no remains of the sections of the town walls that closed off the landward gap NW of the castle or of the riverside sections, but a considerable length survives on the SW side of the town, where there is a retaining wall rising about 4m above the water meadow between it and the river to a wall-walk serving as a pavement to a road behind it. One small square tower three storeys high survives on this section.

Until it was rebuilt c1832 to serve as a theatre a building 30m long by 9m wide occupied "all the space between Cross Hill, St John's Hill, Murivance or Swan Hall and Shoplache" (grid reference SJ 490124). This seems to have been a much altered relic of a house which John de Charlton was licensed by Edward II to embattle in 1325. Any ancient features surviving the 1830s rebuilding were destroyed during another rebuilding of c1905.

SIBDON CARWOOD CASTLE   SO 435818

A 17th century house built by the Corbets and altered by the Flemings in the 18th century and castellated by the Holdens in the early 19th century probably stands on the site of "Shepeton Corbet Castel" seen by John Leland c1540.

SMETHCOTT CASTLE   SO 449994

West of church are slight traces of a motte with a small D-shaped bailey 50m by 35m to the south. Excavations in 1956-7 revealed a ditch, traces of wooden buildings, small circular masonry structures and pottery of the period c1200-50. The site was probably abandoned after the manor passed to the Burnells c1270.

STAPLETON CASTLE   SJ 471044 & 457035

Beside the churchyard is a mound rising 3.5m to a summit 20m across. To the SW of the village is a farm with buildings of the 16th, 17th and later centuries standing on a platform above a moat which is now dry. On the north side the retaining wall is only rough rubble but on the south side it is formed of large blocks with a battered plinth, probably the remains of a 14th century mansion which was built by the Stapleton family, members of which were sheriffs of Shropshire in 1391 and 1441, and knights of the shire in 1421. It passed to the Leightons, who in 1614 leased it to Lord Egerton. From about that time it became just a farmhouse, although an old picture shows it as having a timber-framed gatehouse. The Egertons later became full owners and in the 18th century sold the house to the Powys family.

The fine base of former moated mansion at Stapleton   *Town Wall at Shrewsbury*

STOKESAY CASTLE   SO 436817   E

The de Lacy family held the manor of Stoke at the time of Domesday Book (1086). In the early 12th century one of them granted the manor to Theodoric de Say. The earliest part of the existing house is the thinly-walled north tower of the early 13th century, a structure of no military value. Stokesay passed by exchange to John Verdun c1250 and then to the de Grays. The hall and solar date from soon after 1281 when the manor was purchased by the rich wool merchant Lawrence de Ludlow. He also built the south tower and the curtain wall which formerly enclosed the courtyard, which were licensed by Edward I in 1291 and probably complete when Lawrence died in 1296. Stokesay passed by marriage from the de Ludlows to the Vernons c1500 and in 1570 was sold to the Mainwarings. In 1616 it was acquired by Sir Thomas Baker and Sir Richard Francis, only to be sold to Dame Elizabeth Craven in 1620. Her son, William, Lord Craven, refurbished Stokesay as a possible residence for Elizabeth, daughter of James I, wife of the Elector Palatine and mother of Prince Rupert. In the Civil War Stokesay was garrisoned as an outpost of Royalist Ludlow but in 1645 it was surrendered to a Parliamentary force at the second summons without enduring a siege, being untenable against cannon. Despite this it was still considered necessary to pull down the curtain wall to courtyard level. The place was then leased to the Baldwins but after the early 18th century it was occupied only by tenant farmers and began to decay. The late 17th century additions made by the Baldwins were demolished in 1840 and the rest was restored by the Allcrofts, who purchased Stokesay in 1869. Since the early 1990s it has been maintained by English Heritage.

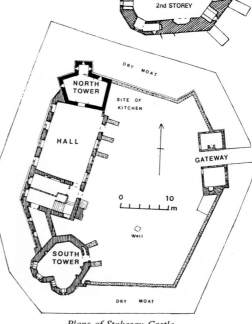

The South Tower at Stokesay

Plans of Stokesay Castle

Stokesay Castle

The timber-framed gatehouse is of two storeys and an attic and stands on a stone base. Ornate but of no military value, it is probably of late 16th century date, it must have replaced a stone gatehouse. The passage is flanked by a pair of almost square rooms walled with closely spaced vertical timbers with fireplaces in brick stacks. On the overhanging upper storey the vertical timbers are wider apart with lozenges between them, whilst a bay window projects out towards the courtyard. The attic has side gables in the middle with windows. The courtyard was originally surrounded by a wall with wall-walk about 3m above courtyard level and 7m above the bottom of the moat. One small fragment remains complete east of the South Tower, but the rest is now just a retaining wall for the inner face of the moat with a modern parapet at courtyard level. Several timber-framed buildings in the court, including a kitchen east of the North Tower and a chamber block east of the solar, have gone, but a well still lies in the middle.

The hall is a lofty and noble apartment of four bays with on each side tall transomed windows of two cusped lights with a plain circle over, set in embrasures with seats. There was no glass in these windows, which are still closed with shutters. The southern window in the west wall was altered when a tall doorway was put in here by a tenant farmer, but the others are intact, apart from 19th century rebuilding of some of the gables above them. There is a shorter fourth window at the north end of the west wall and there may originally have been a similar window over the entrance at the Ne corner. The buttresses flanking the entrance and on the South Tower are 19th century additions. The hall had an open fire in the middle of the floor, for which opening in the roof must have been provided. The present roof is a late medieval remodelling of the original 13th century one. It is possible that the hall was once divided by rows of timber posts into a nave and side aisles.

The gatehouse at Stokesay Castle

Steps from the hall lead into the basement of the pentagonal North Tower. This room has narrow lancet windows with shutters and contains a well. It was probably a pantry. The two upper storeys reached by an open stair rising from the NW corner of the hall contained living rooms with small bedrooms partitioned off in the small square turret projecting out from the north corner. The top storey has a fine fireplace of the 1290s but the overhanging timber framed walls to the north are probably later.

South of the hall is the solar block. This contained a wine cellar below courtyard level, a living room (later subdivided) at hall level, and the lord's private room above. The latter was used as a dining room in the 17th century and has wall panelling of that period and a fine Flemish overmantel on the chimneybreast. This room was reached only by an external stair and on the building can be seen the mark of its penthouse house. Access to the hall from the foot of the stair is by a lobby at the east end of the lower living room, probably an original arrangement. The small rooms between the solar block and the South Tower were probably for the use of servants.

Stokesay Castle

Interior of the North Tower at Stokesay Castle

The South Tower is an irregularly shaped polygonal building containing a cellar and two upper storeys of bedrooms for the use of the family and their guests. This structure is a sort of tower house, militarily independent of the rest of the house, although its walls are only about 1.5m thick and it was more a status symbol than a fortress. The upper storeys were at one time divided by timber partitions, but it is uncertain whether this was the original arrangement. The basement doorway could be a later insertion and the main entrance is by means of a bridge from the top of the solar stair to a second storey doorway. From there stairs in the wall thickness lead both up and down. A third entrance into the top storey is now blocked up. A flat 19th century roof has replaced the low-pitched original one. There are original battlements with cross-loops and a small lookout turret.

STOKE-UPON-TERN CASTLE   SJ 646276

To the south of the existing manor house lies the site of the house of the Verdon family which passed by marriage to Bartholomew de Burghersh in 1328. It was later held by Henry, Lord Ferrers, Sir Rowland Hill and then the Corbets of Adderley, who fortified it for Parliament in 1644. It seems to have been badly damaged or destroyed during the conflict since when the property was sold in 1668 to William Burrows the conveyance referred to "stone, brick, wood and timber, on the place where the castle had lately stood". There are now only slight traces of the former moat with a scatter of old brick fragments within. When a trench was cut across the site in 1964 part of a "massive drystone wall of sandstone blocks" was revealed. In c1889 the remains were said to measure 250 feet each way, but it is unclear whether this included the width of the moat.

TONG CASTLE   SJ 791069

Little was known about the medieval buildings on this site until it was excavated prior to the new M54 motorway being cut diagonally through the middle of it. Until then the site was a wooded promontory rising above the confluence of two streams to the west. The excavations revealed a complicated sequence of buildings from the 12th century to the 18th century. Remains of all except the last were minimal, and most of them were removed for the motorway. The castle was originally a ringwork 40m by 30m on the end of the promontory, approached from the west over the streams.

Richard de Belmeis, Bishop of London and Viceroy of Salop is thought to have had a castle at Tong in the period 1108-27. The 4m high mound with a summit 49m by 25m which lies to the NE at SO 794080 may be the site of it. In the 1160s Tong passed by marriage to the Zouche family, who walled the ringwork and provided a new east approach, where in the early 13th century they added a large outer bailey. The excavations revealed traces of the east wall of this outer bailey and a probably square gatehouse plus part of the base of a round SE corner tower 7m in diameter, although it is possible these features were connected with the licence to crenellate the "Castro de Tonge" issued by Richard II to Fulk IV de Pembridge in 1381.

Tong was held by the Harcourts from c1250 to c1270 and then passed to the Pembridges. They built a new hall block on an north-south axis immediately east of the former ditch of the inner bailey east wall which had probably been removed by then. The subsequent mansions all had their principal rooms laid out on this axis on the same site, although they had various outbuildings elsewhere. On the south side, close to the former junction of the two baileys traces were found of a room which was thought to be a chapel of c1300, since fragments of stained glass and window tracery were found nearby, although it is orientated north-south.

Tong passed in 1447 to the Vernons of Haddon Hall in Derbyshire and Sir Henry Vernon, who died in 1515, erected a new mansion of brick. The castle was captured by the Royalists in 1644 but seems to have been still intact in 1648, when it was described as "fayre old castle" and was acquired by William Pierrepoint, although in 1763 there is a mention in 1763 of the east wing which was destroyed in the Civil War being rebuilt in brick. In fact the whole building was then rebuilt after the deserted old building was sold in 1760 to George Durant. Designed by Capability Brown this mansion was in an unusual Moorish form of Gothick with two lofty domes. It was abandoned before World War I and was finally demolished in 1954 by the then owner Lord Newport because it was considered dangerous.

Most of the site of the inner bailey has been saved as it lies south of the motorway, although it is now overgrown and closed off. The 5m high retaining walls seem to be mostly 17th century, when this area was landscaped to make a garden. Of earlier buildings there remain a 14th or 15th century well 12.5m deep and foundations of a kitchen thought to have been last used c1300. East of these are remains of the supposed chapel and cellars below outbuildings of the Durant mansion. On the other side of the motorway is a triangle corresponding to the NE corner of the outer bailey, an 18th century ice house at the apex being possibly formed from a medieval corner tower base. There are also foundations of a stable and smithy plus other outbuildings.

Upper Millichope Lodge

TYRLEY CASTLE   SJ 678330

The manor (formerly in Staffordshire) was held by the Pantulf family until c1233, and then by the Botillers or Butlers. Ralph Butler began a stone castle on the site of an older fortress but on his death in 1281 it was referred to as "an unfinished fortalice with a messuage and gardens". A "capital messuage" is mentioned in the 14th century but not in the conveyance of 1524, when the manor was sold, but the name Tyrley Castle was revived for whatever house then stood here after Sir Gilbert Gerard purchased it in 1583. There are slight traces of earthworks on a narrow ridge with a gentle slope to the south and a steep slope at the back towards the River Tern and the town of Market Drayton. The brick 18th century farmhouse incorporates some sandstone blocks. Foundations of a curtain wall and a ditch 5m wide were revealed by excavations in 1884 and 1910.

UPPER MILLICHOPE LODGE   SO 522892

The lodge is a rare example of a small medieval stronghouse, now forming part of a farmhouse. Apparently without any outer defences, it contained just a single living room-cum-bedroom over a storage basement, and on the evidence of the upper windows is of the period c1280-1300. It was probably the dwelling of the King's Forester of The Long Forest. Because of the unpopularity of the strict forest laws the holder of such a post may have needed a home that could not be easily broken into or burnt down by poachers. The 1.8m thick walls may have originally supported a wall-walk and parapet but at present timber-framed gables support a roof rising directly off the outer edge of the walls.

The building measures 12.4m by 8.1m and has in the NW wall, facing the farmyard, a round-headed lower doorway with ballflower ornamentation. This must date from c1315-45 but the stones appear to be reset from elsewhere, this entire wall having been refaced at the lower level and rebuilt much thinner on the upper level. As a result of this a stair in the west wall has been blocked and superseded by a timber stair inside the corner. Of four narrow window embrasures in the basement two are converted into wider modern windows, and a third has become a doorway. At the south corner on the upper storey is an embrasure now serving as a window but originally probably the only entrance doorway. In the NE and SE walls of the upper storey are straight-headed windows of two-lights separated by a shaft with a base and capital, and having seats in the embrasures. Timber partitions now subdivide both storeys and there are more rooms in the roof and a later back wing.

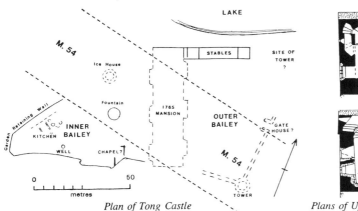
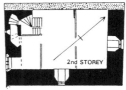

Plan of Tong Castle   *Plans of Upper Millichope Lodge*

WATTLESBOROUGH CASTLE   SJ 355126

At the time of Domesday Book (1086) Wattlesborough was held by Roger Fitz Corbet as a tenant of Roger de Montgomery. The Corbets constructed a modest square tower keep c1200, It was accompanied by a hall block, probably of later date, and although there are now no traces of outer walls three towers are reported to have been demolished to provide materials for alterations to Loton Park and the repair of the church at Alberbury. Wattlesborough passed by marriage in the 1380s to John la Pole, and c1470 it went to the Leightons. They lived in the castle until Sir Edward Leighton made Loton Park his principal home c1711. Later in the 18th century the existing farmhouse was added south of the keep.

The keep is faced with sandstone ashlar and measures 10m by 9.8m above a battered and chamfered plinth from which rise pilaster corner buttresses. The walls are 2.2m thick above the plinth and are 12m high. The building is partly choked inside with rubbish and debris from the collapsed floors and roof. A drawing published by the Reverend Eyton in the mid 19th century shows the tower covered at about its present height with a pyramidal roof without the long-lost embattled parapet.

It is clear from roof marks that as first built the keep contained just a single pleasant living room over a dark cellar with the walls rising up above the roof to protect it. In the 15th century a bedroom was created in the old roof space and three windows (one of two lights), and a fireplace were then inserted at this level. The cellar has two blocked doorways towards the farmhouse, one 14th century, the other later. The only access to the room above was by a ladder and trapdoor and the two windows at this level are later insertions. The room above formed a private chamber opening off the adjacent hall on the site of the farmhouse. Towards it opened the only original doorway, now blocked. All four walls have windows, three of which, all now blocked, are original Late Norman windows of two rectangular lights under a round-headed outer order. Until a fireplace was provided in the 15th century heating must have been by means of brazier on the floor with a smoke outlet in the roof. In the east corner is a spiral stair to the top and the north corner contains a dog-leg passage to a latrine with overhung the face of the wall.

Wattlesborough Castle

  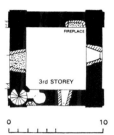 

1st STOREY   2nd STOREY   3rd STOREY   SECTION

Plans and section of the keep at Wattlesborough

0 ————— 10
metres

WEM CASTLE   SJ 511288

All that remains of a castle built by the Pantulf family is a mutilated mound lying immediately west of the church. The mound was 7m high until material from it was removed in the late 18th century, and the highest part now only stands 3m above the ditch. Hugh Pantulf gave the village of Sleap Magna to Richard de Slepe "for his help in building Wem Castle" a possible record of rebuilding in stone during King John's reign. The material remained from the mound certainly included several cart loads of stone, although they could have been mound core materials, rather than the footings of long-destroyed buildings. The castle passed by marriage to the Botilers or Butlers in the 1230s but was ruinous by 1290. It must have been repaired for in 1314 Hugh Fitz Aer held the castle as a tenant of William de Botiler on condition that he provided one man with a lance who was to remain in the castle to attend the fire even if the rest of the garrison went outside. The castle passed to the de Audleys in 1459. Wem may have had a protective bank and ditch in the later medieval period. The town was fortified by Parliament in 1643 and certainly then had a rampart of earth and wood. A Royalist force under Lord Capel failed to capture it before the work was completed.

WHITCHURCH CASTLE   SJ 526403 & 559424

A motte is said to have stood in the town centre until the late 19th century. Either it or the large mound of Pan Castle, 2km to the SW, was the site of a castle founded by William de Warenne, and which later passed to a junior branch of the family, the Fitz Ranulfs. William Fitz Ranulf was given 10 marks by the crown towards repairs to his castle of "Album Monasterium" in 1199. It reverted to William de Warenne in 1240 and later passed to Robert le Strange. Pan Castle consists of an irregularly shaped mound 53, by 47m on top rising up to 5m above its ditch and having a large outer enclosure about 160m by 150m on the south with a ditch on the south and west, still partly water filled, and also a rampart on the south. The le Stranges probably abandoned this site in favour of the moated platform about 40m square at Blakemere beside a lake east of the town. Here probably lay the manor house which Fulk le Strange was licenced to crenellate by Edward II in 1322, although there is a possible alternative moated site just north of the town. It passed to the Talbots c1370, one of whom was made Earl of Shrewsbury in 1442 for his services in France. The house at Blakemere was sold in 1590 and was then rebuilt and the moat cleaned out. It was "almost quite ruinated" in 1695, probably because of damage sustained during the Civil War, and stone is said to have been taken from it for the rebuilding of the parish church in 1712-13.

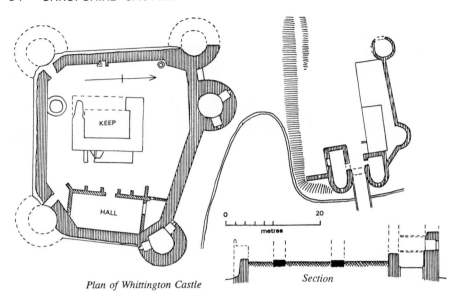

Plan of Whittington Castle　　　　　　　　*Section*

WHITTINGTON CASTLE　　SJ 326312　　F

This castle is first mentioned in 1138 when it was fortified by William Peverel against King Stephen. It was probably built by his uncle William Peverel of Dover who had been granted Whittington by Henry I after it was forfeited by Robert de Bellesme. The younger William was forfeited in 1153 for his part in the poisoning of Ranulf, Earl of Chester, and in 1164 Henry II granted it to Geoffrey de Vere, whose main interest lay elsewhere, although he was married to Isabel de Say of Clun. However in 1165 the castle was given to Roger de Powys and in 1173 he was granted aid for its repair. Roger was succeeded by his sons Meredith and Meyric but in 1204 Whittington was acquired by Fulk Fitz Warine, a descendant of the Peverels. He is assumed to have built the keep prior to 1215 when he was in rebellion against King John, and the minimal remains suggest it may have been dismantled or left unfinished. Fulke made his peace with the regents acting for the young Henry III and in 1221 was licensed to "build the castle up only as much as was essential to fortify it against the Welsh". Building work on the curtain walls and towers of the inner ward was probably still in progress when the castle was captured by the Welsh in 1223.

The castle held out against an attack by Owain Glyndwr in 1405. On the death of the last of nine successive Fulk Fitz Warines in 1415 Whittington passed by marriage to Sir William Bouchier, later Earl of Bath. After his execution by Henry VI the castle was granted to the Earl of Stafford. The castle was decayed but nearly entire when surveyed in 1545 and was later granted by Queen Mary to the Earl of Arundel. It then fell into ruin and was robbed of its materials. One of the eastern towers of the inner ward fell into the moat c1760 and stones from the west tower of the inner gatehouse and adjacent west wall were used to repair the road from Whittington to Halston. Another tower in 1898 provided material for the repair of the outer gatehouse. In the 1970s the walls and earthworks were cleared of undergrowth and debris and made accessible to the public. The outer gatehouse still remains habitable.

Whittington Castle

The castle originally consisted of a small motte with an inner bailey to the east and two further baileys to the north, the whole being surrounded by wet moats. Around the site of the earlier keep erected in the middle of the inner bailey Fulk Fitz Warine created a small but strongly fortified inner ward by encasing the platform with walls up to 2m thick rising straight out of the moat with large round corner towers. Two of these were placed close together at the NW corner with a gateway between them. The curtain walls stand in a defaced condition up to courtyard level, and the base of the NE tower contains D-shaped room with two embrasures for arrow-loops. The other towers all contained completely circular rooms although externally they had straight faces to the court. Only traces remain of the two southern towers, and only part of the basement of the west tower of the gatehouse, but the east tower of the gatehouse still stands three storeys high, the middle storey being at courtyard level. There are several cross-shaped arrow loops in this tower, and a blocked postern at moat level facing east. There is also a doorway to the former wall-walk, showing it was about 3.6m above the court and 7m high above the moat.

Whittington Castle

The keep measured 15.1m by 11.6m over walls 2.6m to 2.8m thick, the west wall being missing. The keep had a chamfered plinth and was similar in size to Fitz Warine's other keep at Alberbury. The main chamber was raised over a cellar and was reached by an external stair on the east side. On the east side of the courtyard are foundations of a hall 15.3m long by 7.3m wide internally. The ashlar wall facing the court is buttressed and probably of the early 14th century. On the south side of the court is an oven and by the west tower of the inner gatehouse is a well.

West of the inner ward is the motte, now reduced to about 4m high. Neither it or the northern baileys were ever walled in stone, but there was a small outer ward created in the SE corner of the NE bailey. This was just large enough to contain outbuildings such as stables and workshops for which there was no room in the inner ward. This outer ward is much less stoutly built and neither its walls, towers or two-towered gatehouse have walling greater than 1m thick. It is better preserved because the outer gatehouse and the timber framed building behind it remained in use after the inner ward fell into ruin. The bridge over the moat, which still contains water on this side, and the gatehouse battlements are not of great age. Each gatehouse tower has one badly worm cross-loop like those in the surviving inner gatehouse tower and the archway between them was closed by a two-leaved door and a drawbridge.

SURVIVING MOATED SITES IN SHROPSHIRE

Plans of moats marked * appear on page 12. There were once moats at Alberbury Priory SJ 375151, Battlefield College SJ 513172, and Ludstone Hall SO 800945

Acton Burnell SJ 529019
Alcaston SO 459870
Belswardine* SJ 609025
Bearstone SJ 724394
Bower SO 555722
Calverhall SJ 603377
Cherrington SJ 666202
Cleeton St Mary* SO 608791
Cloverley Hall SJ 612372
Fauls SJ 586327
Gadlas SJ 373371
Hadnall* SJ 522199
Hanwood* SJ 447094
Highfields SJ 510309
Humphreston* SJ 814050
Hunkington SJ 565141
Hurst SJ 355073
Ightfield Hall SJ 600394
Leafields SO 646725
Lea Hall SJ 583385
Lea Head SJ 760422
Lower Grounds SJ 594159
Lower Newton SJ 487313
Middle Morrey SJ 624403
Middleton* SO 296987
New Marton SJ 340345
Newstreet Lane SJ 627373

Northwood SJ 493311
Old Park Farm SJ 714005
Petton* SJ 443265
Pool Hall SO 768838
Shackerley SJ 814064
Shawbury* SJ 561212
Shifnal SJ 746074
Snitton SO 557754
Soudley SJ 731297
Stanwardine SJ 427277
Startlewood SJ 387206
Syllenhurst SJ 725427
The Isle* SJ 457167
The Lees SJ 668263
Thonglands SO 549891
Uppington SJ 592087
Upton Cressett SO 656924
Watling St Grange SJ 722113
Wem SJ 599305
Westhope* SO 467859
Whitley Grange SJ 4543096
Whixall SJ 504337
Willaston SJ 597360
Wistanstow* SO 422861
Wollerton Wood SJ 609311
Woodhouse SO 647771

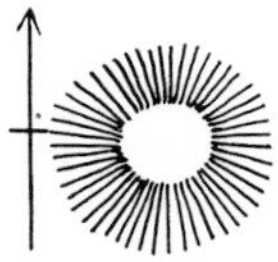

Gwarthlow Motte

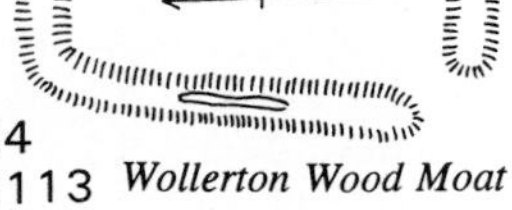

Wollerton Wood Moat

Wotherton Motte

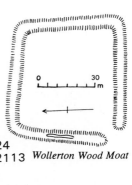

OTHER NORMAN EARTHWORKS IN SHROPSHIRE

BICTON SO 289826 Small damaged mound 2m high, 14m across on top, with ditch 10m wide and 1.5m deep.

BINWESTON SO 302041 Farmhouse on stump of motte described as 4.5m high and 15m across on top c1908. Surrounding moat fed from a stream.

BRETCHEL SJ 337117 Damaged motte rising 3m to summit 7.5m across by farm.

BROADWARD SO 394766 D-shaped mound rising 3m to summit 16m by 10m by River Clun. A second mound once lay close to the SW.

BROCKTON SO 580937 East of the village is a mound rising 2m above a partly wet moat to an overgrown summit 16m across.

BROMLOW SJ 320024 Rock scarped into motte 4m high and 7.5m across on top with ditch except above drop to the east. Outer bank to the south.

BRYN-Y-CASTELL SJ 304340 Oval motte 2m high with traces of a bailey to west.

BUCKNELL SO 356739 Small damaged motte rising 4m to summit 7.5m across.

CHIRBURY SO 258985 Platform 58m square up to 4m high beside stream. Excavated 1958. No finds of interest. Manor held by de Salnervilles and then the de Bollars, reverting to the crown by the 1220s.

CHURCH PREEN SO 538976 Castleyard is said to be the site of a castle.

CLUNGUNFORD SO 395788 Mound 3m high, top 15m across, by river NE church.

COLEBATCH SO 320871 Motte by stream rising 5m to a summit 4m across.

COLSTEY SO 303841 Small mound north of Colstey Farm destroyed in 1960s.

CULMINGTON SO 497822 Mound rising 3m above partly water-filled ditch to summit 15m across. Bailey 35m to SW. L-shaped enclosure to NE.

DUDSTON SO 245974 The buildings of East Dudston Farm cut into mound 4m high with overgrown summit 12m long.

EATON SO 374895 Barrow adapted as motte 3m high. Damaged by roadworks.

EDGTON SO 401868 Triangular platform 70m by 55m with rampart to north and east and drop to west. Possibly the "old castle" mentioned in 1250.

FITZ SJ 448178 Mound by churchyard, partly removed 1860 to enlarge adjacent farmhouse and dug into on east and west sides in 1901, revealing charcoal.

GWARTHLOW SO 252955 Motte rising 5m to a summit 12m by 9m. Ditch on east.

HARDWICK SO 368906 Overgrown mound rising 3m to summit 16m across.

HINSTOCK SJ 690260 No remains of castle site marked on old maps.

HISLAND SJ 317275 4m high motte, with summit 12m by 9m. By farm.

HOCKLETON SO 274999 South of bridge and farm is a 3.5m high mound with traces of D-shaped bailey platform 35m by 18m to the NE.

HOPE SJ 344023 A small oval motte rising 3m to a summit 5m long.

KINTON SJ 370194 Mound rising 2m to summit 13m across. SE side cut away.

LEE BROCKHURST SJ 546273 Mound NE of church removed c1962. Site built over.

LITTLE NESS SJ 407197 The Late Norman church lies in a probably bailey platform 45m by 40m serving an adjacent mound rising 5m to a summit just 3m across. Excavations c1870 revealed animal bones and burnt timber.

LOWER DOWN SO 336846 Motte damaged by removal of gravel for roadworks but still 3m high and 15m across on top. Traces formerly visible of stonework.

MARCHAMLEY SJ 594294 Mound with 18th century brick building may be site of the "fortalice" mentioned in 1223.

MARCHE HALL SJ 243107 Ringwork 35m by 26m with ditch 1m deep on west.

MARTON SJ 290026 5m high motte has almost gone. Bailey 55m by 35m still has ditch and rampart on north and ditch on the west.

MIDDLEHOPE SO 499886 To the east of a lane are traces of a mound and its ditch. To the west of the lane is a circular platform 15m by 13m.

MINTON SO 432906 Motte rising 5m to overgrown summit 13m across.

NEWCASTLE SO 244820 Worn down motte 2m high by River Clun.

OAKLANDS SJ 290370 Oval motte rising 3m from ditch on south to summit 25m by 10m. Steep drop to River Ceiriog on north, Chirk being opposite.

PENNERLEY SO 351994 A low mound with a summit about 10m across.

PETTON SJ 441262 Mound up to 3m high, 10m across on top, SE of church.

PICKTHORNE SO 669840 Low platform 56m by 34m may be site of a residence of the Baskerville family mentioned c1284.

PONTFADOG SJ 292211 Low mound in marsh by stream south of Oswestry.

RITTON SO 345977 Crescent-shaped rampart 3.5m high about 10m wide ditch 1m deep cuts off court 32m by 28m on promontory above stream. Traces of bailey 170m east-west by 80m wide to south.

RORRINGTON SJ 303004 Mound with sloping summit 14m across, 2.5m high on east but higher on the west.

SOULTON SJ 546303 Mound rising 3m above ditch 15th wide to summit 20m by 16m. By a stream NE of Soulton Hall. Seat of Suleton family in 13th century.

TENBURY WELLS SO 594686 Mound near Teme rising 3m to summit 6m across.

WEST FELTON SJ 340252 Mound west of church rising 3m above partly wet ditch formerly with stone lining to summit 35 in diameter. Smaller mound 10m across on top and 1.5m high lies in the centre.

WHITSBURN HILL SJ 328029 Ringwork 37m across with ditch 10m wide, 1m deep.

WILCOTT SJ 379185 Tree-clad ringwork 3 to 4m high and 28m across.

WILDERLEY SJ 433017 SW of the hall is an overgrown motte 4.5m high above its ditch and 12m across on top with a bailey 60m square to the east and traces of a second bailey 60m by 30m beyond.

WILLASTON SJ 597359 Tree-clad 2m high mound, 15m across on top.

WILMINGTON SJ 298021 A motte 4m high with an uneven summit 7.5m across lies at one end of a pear-shaped bailey with a rampart on the south. The walling on the mound summit is probably a relic of a later summer house.

WINSBURY SO 246984 Motte 6m high with top 30m across partly removed c1870, rest removed 1961 after excavations revealing a ditch 4m deep and 13th century pottery. Seat of de Winsbury family from before 1127 to after 1315.

WOLLASTON SJ 328123 Church on site of D-shaped bailey 110m by 60m with motte 6m high with summit 10m across. A worn ringwork 45m across lies to the SW at SJ 324120.

WOOLSTASTON SO 450985 Mound west of church rises 3m to summit 13m across. Traces of bailey platform 55m by 30m extend to the NE. Excavations in the bailey found 12th and 13th century pottery.

WORSLEY SO 461959 Oval mound 3m high and 8m by 14m on top of Castle Hill.

WOTHERTON SJ 283007 Motte by stream, 3m high to summit 7m across.

WROXETER SJ 562081 Possible site of castle of the Fitz Alans. Masonry found in 1859 could have been either Roman or medieval.

YOCKLETON SJ 396103 Above a stream NE of the church is a 4m high motte with an oddly shaped summit 25m by 12m.

Mound at Belan Bank (see page 48)